The Future of Fashion is Now

museum   van
boijmans beuningen

Contents

Foreword

Fashion has undergone a profound change. All over the world, a new generation of idealistic and socially engaged designers are viewing society and the fashion system with a critical eye. Inspired by leading innovators, a symbiotic and sustainable image of fashion has emerged in which life is consciously expressed in terms of a new fashion identity. This is fashion that is personal, oriented towards society and the community, socially conscious and made with the new materials and techniques of our age. Fashion that communicates. Fashion for our time.

It's a time of exponential population growth, globalisation, climate change, the repositioning of West and East, the redistribution of raw materials and spheres of influence and the collision of ideologies. Conflicts arise in which the individual always gets short shrift. It's a time that is inciting young designers to innovate and to redefine what fashion is. Fashion as a global social plea for freedom, opportunity, self-development and engagement. Fashion against the system.

Five years after *The Art of Fashion*, which featured fashion that borders on the visual arts, Museum Boijmans Van Beuningen is once again taking stock. Like five years ago, both the exhibition and the book offer detailed insight into what is going on internationally in the fashion laboratories, in the designer studios. *The Future of Fashion is Now* is an exhibition based on the knowledge of a company of eminent fashion authorities and fashion scholars from around the world who have shared their most up-to-date information with us.

I would like to thank the writer, art activist and patron Han Nefkens, whose Han Nefkens Fashion on the Edge initiative has for many years made it possible for Museum Boijmans Van Beuningen to serve as a podium for the exhibition and propagation of experimental developments in fashion. Guest curator José Teunissen, all the scouts, advisors and designers involved in this intercontinental project: thank you for your insight, knowledge and time. I hope the freedom and inspiration you engender reaches all the inhabitants of our earth.

Sjarel Ex
Director Museum Boijmans Van Beuningen

installations that show their sources of inspiration but are not suited for the commercial collection. So I decided to help a number of them, and in exchange for my help the dress or installation will become part of my collection and will go to a museum on long-term loan. What I find so fascinating about these projects is that the most extraordinary fantasies are brewing in the heads of so many designers. I want to see those fantasies. I want to help bring them to life.

So now here I am, amidst all the tulle and silk and the silver-plated accessories, silver-plating part of the dresses being the theme of the collection. What gave Viktor&Rolf the idea was the custom of silver-plating a baby's first shoes.

By the next day I'm the owner of *Fabiana*, a dress with a full silver skirt, a silver-plated corset with a Viktor&Rolf bow and a silver-plated veil that covers the wearer's face.

November 2008, Amsterdam

In the circular room at Platform 21 an installation by Christophe Coppens is being shown. *No References* is a sewing studio placed in a theatrical set, where the pastel-coloured objects serve no function, although they do form a single unit. All the elements are related: heads from which a piece of fabric is protruding, casings for legs and arms. The work in its entirety is inscrutable, but it's enchantingly beautiful.

Christophe is the first winner of the Han Nefkens Fashion Award. From now on, this prize – which consists of 25,000 euros, 15,000 of which is to be used for the creation of a new work – will be awarded every two years to a young designer who is exploring the area between fashion and art. I want to give a chance to designers who have already shown what they can do but haven't yet had a major breakthrough.

March 2009, London

I'm sitting at a big, round table in a restaurant in the trendy Shoreditch district, where José and I have agreed to meet with three designers who have been commissioned to make something for *The Art of Fashion*. The exhibition is to open in September at Museum Boijmans Van Beuningen, which has now become the home base of the Fashion on the Edge initiative. The designers come to discuss their proposals individually. Hussein Chalayan wonders whether water or moss should be added to the terrarium with the revolving figure he's designing. Anna-Nicole Ziesche isn't sure about the background of her film: should it be white, or would some striking colour show up better? And Naomi Filmer wants to know if she should produce all five of the sculptures in her *Breathing Volume* project in bronze.

Mostly I listen. I don't yet have the confidence to offer my opinion. I'm a beginner in the fashion world, but at least I know more than I did five years ago. In the past few years we've purchased works by well-known and lesser known designers. We've also commissioned various works, and I was able to follow the entire creative process, from idea to concrete object. I see how designers wrestle to find the right form for their ideas, just like the artists whose works I commission in collaboration with museums, just like myself when I write. And I see that the form almost always changes during the process, just as it does with me.

After the discussions we all eat lunch together: spaghetti, turbot with lemon sauce, tomato salad and wine. This is what I'm doing it for, I realise, to sit around the table with these people and talk about what moves us, the pleasure of working together on the same goal, our exhibition. I pour myself another glass.

January 2010, Rotterdam
Today is the last day of *The Art of Fashion*, and a photographer wants to take a picture of me for a newspaper article. It's after five when he leaves, and the visitors are gone as well. I'm standing alone among the works of Walter Van Beirendonck, Louise Bourgeois, Salvador Dalí, Maison Martin Margiela, Comme des Garçons, Elsa Schiaparelli and many others. The attendant switches off the light and says I've really got to leave the gallery now. When he shuts the door behind me, I take my phone out of my pocket and call José: I have an idea for a new exhibition.

September 2012, Rotterdam
Again I'm being photographed, this time for the installation by the South Korean designer Rejina Pyo. The sleek lines and the colours of her dresses remind me of Mondrian and De Stijl, but three-dimensionally stylised. Rejina is the third winner of the Han Nefkens Fashion Award. After the American artist Charles LeDray won the second Han Nefkens Fashion Award in 2010 with his installation *MENS SUITS*, José and I decided to find out what young designers in non-Western countries and in Eastern Europe were doing. We purchased work by the Japanese designer Pyuupiru, among other things, and began to make plans for the new exhibition. Besides work by well-established designers we also want to

show some up-and-coming talent from around the world. The work we acquired or commissioned over the last five years, along with dozens of borrowed works, will come together to make up *The Future of Fashion is Now*.

April 2013, Amsterdam

On a rainy Thursday morning, José and I are sitting in the small office of Superheroes website builders to talk about creating a site for *The Future of Fashion is Now*. We want to show how the exhibition is progressing, but we also want to create a platform where young designers from around the world can exchange their ideas and experiences. Filled with admiration, I listen to the young staff members from Superheroes and Museum Boijmans Van Beuningen come up with all sorts of innovative ideas. We want to launch a discussion on the site and they're supplying possible subjects, such as the role of the body in fashion and the relationship between fashion and nature. They ask whether fantasy is kitsch or whether it creates an environment in which reality can be displayed in a different way; they want designers to start talking about where the balance lies between a garment's conceptual and visual side and about whether fashion becomes increasingly personal.

The website builders also make room for the profiles of our sixteen 'scouts': fashion experts from around the world, each of whom have recommended three designers from their own country or region for the exhibition. An international jury will choose six winners from these designers, and each winner will be commissioned to create a work. We want to show the creative process of these six on the site by means of text, sketches, photographs and films.

Two months later our website goes online.

October 2013, Amsterdam

Set out on a table in a room in the Conservatorium Hotel are dozens of dossiers of young designers who have been proposed by our scouts. The editor-in-chief of *Vogue Netherlands*, Karin Swerink, the Greek artist and fashion curator Vassilis Zidianakis, Viktor&Rolf, José and I are all bending over the drawings and photos of the various works. There are designs for clothing made from unusual materials such as ramie and organic cotton, batiked and dyed clothing, works that suggest social engagement, and fashion as a reflection of an environment or a desire. The emphasis is almost always on traditional methods and sustainability. A remarkably large number of designers poke fun at the fashion industry. The dossiers clearly show that young designers have a different and often surprising take on fashion, and that this individual interpretation is going strong, even in non-Western countries. It gives me great pleasure to travel all over the world, as it were, from this little room.

We take the dossiers that remain after the pre-selection and spread them out on the floor. We inspect them from up close and then take a step back, as you see people doing with paintings in museums. We change the order, remove some of the dossiers and finally agree on the winners. We still don't know what they're going to make, but from what we've seen in the dossiers we're confident that their work is going to be exceptional.

May 2014, Barcelona

I'm sitting in my study behind the computer and see e-mails with sketches, drawings, photos and films that were made by the designers and are coming in from Peru, China, England, Australia, Poland and the Netherlands. Every sketch, every photo shows the next step in the creation process, and the exhibition begins to take shape in my head. The quality of the works is high and there's enormous variety: from social projects to crocheted clothing.

I exult over the thought that in several months thousands of people will be able to see what is now being made, that we'll be able to look at the works from so close up that we'll almost be able to smell them. And there's no doubt in my mind that when the doors of the Bodon Gallery close at the end of *The Future of Fashion is Now*, José and I will already be making plans for the next exhibition in 2019.

The Future of
Fashion is Now

Longing for a Future Society

José Teunissen

'... today's artists do not so much express the tradition from which they come as the path they take between that tradition and the various contexts they traverse, and they do this by performing acts of transition.'[1]

Introduction

Since the beginning of this millennium, fashion has ceased being a strictly Western phenomenon. Fashion designers can hail from any continent and are no longer required to relocate to Paris, London or Milan to be discovered and to build up a career. They can achieve an international reputation right in their own country by means of web shops, blogs, social media and local fashion weeks, without the intermediate step of discovery in Paris or London by fashion journalists and buyers.[2]

Many newcomers in the fashion world did not grow up with a knowledge of Western fashion history and the related movements, such as postmodernism, conceptualism and modernism. Until recently, any added value they had to offer was mainly put down to the fact that they were tapping into their own traditions and craftsmanship and transforming them into fashion. In the exhibition *Global Fashion Local Tradition* (2005) and the publication of the same name, it was explained that by combining traditional craftsmanship with their own taste and style, non-Western designers were imparting a 'national' identity to their work, and as a result they were seen as unique and 'authentic'.[3] Several studies have also appeared on this subject.[4]

Global Fashion Local Tradition: On the Globalisation of Fashion, 2005

Interestingly, the notion of 'national identity' has been an essential aspect of fashion ever since the eighties. The fashion press never fail to mention the origins of each designer they cover (including Western designers), and a series of fashion analysts have tried to explain what this signifies.[5] The Antwerp Six were branded 'Belgian' thanks to a sophisticated marketing strategy conducted by the government during the eighties, and Dutch designers such as Viktor&Rolf and Alexander van Slobbe were given the title 'Dutch Modernists' because they have a conceptual design

Alexander van Slobbe,
SO, autumn/winter
1999-2000

Comme des Garçons
– Rei Kawakubo,
autumn/winter
1983-1984

identity that is recognisably Dutch.[6] Issey Miyake, Yohji Yamamoto and Comme des Garçons represented a Japanese fashion identity that has its origins in the tradition of the kimono.[7] But this might also be a matter of *auto-exotic gaze*: a representative of a non-Western culture looking at his own culture from a Western perspective, which he then translates into an 'exotic' product for the Western market.[8]

Origins and cultural traditions are still important in the twenty-first century, but the new generation of fashion designers have a different way of employing such characteristics: they explicitly link local styles and craftsmanship with new technologies and new notions of what fashion and clothing might mean in society, both now and in the future, and they do this in a quite natural way. Today's designers are no longer searching for an 'authentic' style that references their origins; their main concern is to critique the present fashion system with its consumerism and its excessive and barely sustainable production methods and to embrace new technologies, resulting in new ways of imagining fashion.

Beyond origins

According to curator and theoretician Nicolas Bourriaud, the fixation on origins – on *roots* – and the related fixation on 'authenticity' and an original 'identity' has to do with the postmodern thinking that was emerging in the 1970s.[9] Postmodernism meant that everything (including culture) was to be interpreted in political terms and reduced to place and origin, and thereby to gender and ethnicity. At the same time, the far-reaching globalisation of the past thirty years has reinforced the fixation on authenticity, identity and origins even more. Because of the enormous overproduction of objects, images and information that have become accessible to everyone via the internet, a homogenisation of cultures and languages has taken place. In reaction, strong movements of disengagement have developed, with people clinging frantically to their own culture and identity. On the other hand, we are also seeing an increase in *creolisation*: cultures and identities blending together without any one of them claiming a dominant position.[10] 'Of course,' says Bourriaud in *The Radicant*, 'roots are important, but it is roots that make individuals suffer; in our globalized world, they persist like phantom limbs after amputation, causing pain impossible to treat, since they affect something that no longer exists.'[11] Origin, authenticity and identity are still important concepts in the world of art and design, but they are no longer being used to advance a 'national identity'. The youngest generation of designers deploy origin, craftsmanship, tradition and identity as fragments for sketching out an image of the future.

A new visual language and new forms

These fragments of identity acquire meaning in the context of the *project*, in which the focus is not on the product but on the process. In the working process of today's designer, new forms of presentation are essential. Most designers show their 'innovative' vision not by means of a single garment or product but by inviting the observer to accompany them throughout the entire design and thought process, which is presented by means of storytelling and future scenarios. The fashion campaign, the catwalk and the fashion magazine are no longer the platform that everyone takes for granted. New presentation sites are being sought out, from empty factories and technology fairs to urban hubs and social networks. Akira Minagawa of the label minä perhonen (Japan) builds poetic stories around particular motifs, which he shows off again and again and reworks in many different forms, such as curtains and upholstery. Elisa van Joolen (the Netherlands) presented the project *11" x 17"* in an Amsterdam dry cleaners shop. Mary Ping of the label Slow and Steady Wins the Race (United States) always organises an exhibition in a gallery or museum to accompany her new, sustainable outfits. Adele Varcoe (Australia) unravels Chanel's

minä perhonen – Akira Minagawa, *Forest Parade*, autumn/winter 2009-2010

Slow and Steady Wins
the Race – Mary Ping,
spring/summer 2009

Adele Varcoe,
Imagining Chanel,
Sydney, 2012

Lucía Cuba, *Artículo 6*,
visual essay *La Espera*
(*The Waiting*), 2013

Lucy + Jorge Orta,
*Nexus Architecture
x 35 – Nexus Type
Opera.tion*, 2001

brand identity by means of a performance, *Imagining Chanel*.
Lucía Cuba (Peru) and Lucy + Jorge Orta (United Kingdom and
Argentina) use their work (*Artículo 6* and *Nexus Architecture*
respectively, both projects from 2012) to create social cohesion,
thereby delivering the political message that such cohesion is
missing in today's society.

'Radicante' identity

A splendid example of a project where the focus is on the
process and not on the final product is *11″ x 17″* by Elisa
van Joolen, in which she plays with the identities of various
fashion brands. Almost every brand has a crew neck sweater
in its collection, and what Van Joolen wants to know is how
you can create a unique, authentic and original product if
everybody else is making the same garment. Van Joolen makes
the question of brand identity visible by asking different
brands to give her samples of their sweaters, which she cuts
into A3-shaped pieces and then frames. For the viewer this is
the beginning of a semiotic exploration: after the fragments
are placed side by side, the differences and similarities in
material and stitch suddenly become apparent, thereby
demonstrating that every brand is different at a materialistic
micro-level. It isn't the final result that's important here – the
framed parts of the sweaters – but what they set in motion:
the search for differences. The *11″ x 17″* project plays with
brand identities and brand characteristics by isolating them
and placing them next to each other, so that different layers

of information are involved.[12] This makes Van Joolen a 'no-madic sign collector', in Bourriaud's terms: 'an inventor of pathways within a cultural landscape and among signs, a nomadic sign gatherer'.[13]

Bourriaud calls this form of identity a *radicant*, like a plant that sends out roots from its stem and propagates in order to keep re-creating its identity. This principle is evident in the *11″ x 17″* project. But in this case it isn't the cultural identity of the maker that renews itself. Van Joolen works with the characteristic marks of a brand's identity and builds a story with them, like an 'intersubjective narrative that unfolds between the subject and the surfaces it traverses, to which

Elisa van Joolen,
11″ x 17″, since 2013

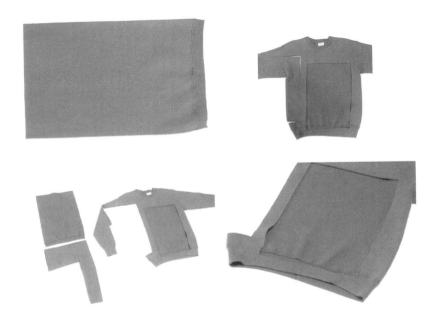

it attaches its roots to produce an installation: one installs oneself. Thus the radicant subject appears as a construction or montage, in other words, as a work born of endless nego-tiation.'[14] In short, here identity is constructed as a series of fragments that tell the story together.

Conclusion: the era of 'altermodern' fashion

In their ideas and manifestations, today's fashion designers show striking similarities with what Bourriaud calls the 'alter-modern artist'. Unlike postmodernism, altermodernism does not concern itself with the past, origins and 'authentic' iden-tity, but with the future, and it is premised on the destination rather than the source. An altermodern designer asks questions about the future: where are we headed in this society? And how can we make a place there for our identity or our origins? So it's not only about the identity of the designer or the artist. The identity of the fashion brand is also being examined, or the identity of the wearer in relation to the identity of the brand, or the relationship of the identity to the environment. 'What I am calling altermodernity thus designates a construction plan that would allow new intercultural connections, the construction of space of negotiation going beyond postmodern multiculturism, which is attached to the origin of discourses and forms rather than to their dynamics.' Artists and fashion designers today take those who look at and/or wear their clothing on a journey and make them partners in their dreams of and longings for a better society. They try to give them an impression of what the world will look like then and what new relationships we have with the fashion products that surround us.

The effects of globalisation have also produced a new aesthetic and a new design language that is no longer searching for an authentic national style or being expressed in terms of regional craftsmanship.[15] Like the altermodern artist, today's fashion designer is someone who brings together a collection of heterogeneous elements to which he or she imparts meaning in an ever-changing context: 'in the infinite text of world'.[16] According to Bourriaud, each designer then becomes a *semionaut* 'accepting the idea that no speech bears the seal of any sort of "authenticity": we are entering the era of universal subtitling.'[17] So designers, too, are doing their best to convert their stories into a universal visual language that is comprehensible to everyone.

That probably explains why fashion has taken on so many new forms. The photo or the outfit alone will no longer suffice; the contents and meaning of the work must also be explained by means of the revealed thought and construction process and the background stories. Performances, films and installations are the ideal media for this work, as are traveller's chronicles and process reports. For this generation of designers, what matters most are not agents, investors, being mentioned in fashion magazines or appearing on the catwalk. Today's designers are making use of the power being generated by globalised culture. Instead of gravitating to the metropolitan power centres they're searching for the local and decentralised places. And it's often the local culture and structure of unique, attractive suburbs of cities like Berlin, Istanbul and

New York (Brooklyn) that provide the most inspiring shopping districts. These are also the places where designers like to settle and establish themselves in a closely-knit community, where they can create new technological or sustainable production methods right in their own neighbourhood. Social media and having their own webshops offer them substantial mobility, as it were: in the networked environment they have at their disposal a worldwide circle of like-minded people, and they capture an international market with a small-scale, sustainable business.

1 Nicolas Bourriaud, *The Radicant*, New York 2009, pp. 51-52.

2 José Teunissen, 'On the Globalisation of Fashion', in: Jan Brand and José Teunissen (eds.), *Global Fashion Local Tradition*, exhibition catalogue, Centraal Museum, Utrecht, Arnhem 2005, pp. 8-23.

3 Brand and Teunissen, 2005 (see note 2).

4 José Teunissen, 'Deconstructing Belgian and Dutch Fashion Dreams. From Global Trends to Local Crafts', in: *Fashion Theory*, 15 (June 2011), no. 2, pp. 137-215, q.v. pp. 157-177; Lise Skov, 'Dreams of Small Nations in a Polycentric Fashion World', in: *Fashion Theory*, 15 (June 2011), no. 2, pp. 137-157.

5 Lise Skov, 'Fashion-Nation: A Japanese Globalization Experience and a Hong Kong dilemma', in: Sandra Niessen, Ann Marie Leshkowich and Carla Jones (eds.), *Re-Orienting Fashion: The Globalisation of Asian Dress*, Oxford 2003; Alison Goodrum, *The National Fabric: Fashion, Britishness, Globalisation*, Oxford 2005; Jennifer Craik, 'Is Australian Fashion and Dress Distinctively Australian?', in: *Fashion Theory*, 13 (2009), pp. 409-441.

6 Javier Gimeno Martinez, 'Fashion, Country and City: The Fashion Industry and the Construction of Collective Identities (1981-2001)', in: Nele Bernheim (ed.), *Symposium 1: Modus Operandi: State of Affairs in Current Research on Belgian Fashion*, ModeMuseum, Antwerp 2008, pp. 17-35; Teunissen, 'Deconstructing Belgian and Dutch Fashion Dreams' (see note 4).

7 Akiko Fukai, 'Japan and Fashion', in: Jan Brand and José Teunissen (eds.), *The Power of Fashion*, Arnhem 2006, pp. 288-314.

8 Dorinne Kondo, *About Face: Performing Race in Fashion and Theatre*, London 1997, p. 58.

9 Bourriaud, 2009 (see note 1), pp. 51-52.

10 Here Bourriaud is referring to the publication by the West Indian writer Edouard Glissant, *Introduction à une poëtique du divers*, Paris 1996, p. 15.

11 Bourriaud, 2009 (see note 1), p. 21.

12 The correspondence Van Joolen carried on with the brands' marketing departments, which is also part of the work, shows how a fashion brand guards the label's identity.

13 Bourriaud, 2009 (see note 1), p. 53.

14 Bourriaud, 2009 (see note 1), p. 55.

15 Bourriaud calls this an altermodern aesthetic.

16 Bourriaud, 2009 (see note 1), p. 4.

17 Bourriaud, 2009 (see note 1), p. 44.

Texts Jos Arts:

Anrealage Kunihiko Morinaga / **Carole Collet / Christophe Coppens / Lucía Cuba / D&K** Ricarda Bigolin and Nella Themelios / **Digest Design Workshop** Dooling Jiang / **Pauline van Dongen / Ying Gao / Hassan Hajjaj / Helen Storey Foundation** Helen Storey / **Pia Interlandi / Eunjeong Jeon / Elisa van Joolen / Hefin Jones / Jacob Kok / Aliki van der Kruijs / Victoria Ledig / Little Shilpa** Shilpa Chavan / **minä perhonen** Akira Minagawa / **Jef Montes / Jum Nakao / Lucy + Jorge Orta / Nuages Gris** Jeroen Teunissen and Dorith Sjardijn / **Sruli Recht / Shao Yen** Shao Yen Chen / **Slow and Steady Wins the Race** Mary Ping / **Lara Torres / Adele Varcoe / Viktor&Rolf**

Texts Hanka van der Voet:

Boundless Zhang Da / **Christoph Broich / Tania Candiani / Hussein Chalayan / Si Chan / Movana Chen / Comme des Garçons** Rei Kawakubo / **Birgit Dieker / Jennifer Gadient / Phyllis Galembo / Craig Green / Imme van der Haak / Iris van Herpen / Forrest Jessee / Mason Jung / Julia Krantz / Wang Lei / Maison Martin Margiela** Martin Margiela / **Olek** Agata Oleksiak / **Minna Palmqvist / mintdesigns** Hokuto Katsui and Nao Yagi / **Antoine Peters / Rejina Pyo / Pyuupiru / Ana Rajcevic / Irina Shaposhnikova / Lilia Yip**

The Future of Fashion is Now

Materiality and Experience

José Teunissen

Craftsmanship, the way a garment is made, the quality of its construction and the physical experience of wearing it are angles of approach that many fashion designers today frequently draw to our attention. This is a new phenomenon. For a long time, fashion was mainly aimed at creating a visual image and a recognisable brand.[1] It had to look good on the catwalk and in the fashion magazines or it had to have 'hang appeal' in the shops. But attention to the product itself – the fabric, the tactile value and the craftsmanship with which the garment was made – became less and less important, partly due to extreme industrialisation and the outsourcing of fashion in the eighties. In the nineties, Martin Margiela was one of the first designers to draw attention to the clothing itself and to the creation process: he made a collection of garments that could be folded back to their original pattern. He and the Japanese designers Rei Kawakubo and Yohji Yamamoto were also among the first to show how time and impermanence left their mark on clothing by playing with the phenomenon of wear and tear as well as with other effects of use. A great deal of attention is also being paid today to the new meanings being generated by innovative production processes.

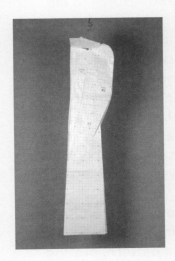

Maison Martin Margiela – Martin Margiela, *Pattern for a long coat*, autumn/winter 1997-1998. Photography: Tom Haartsen

Wearers leave intimate traces behind in their clothing such as smells or 'elbows', giving clothing the aspect of a moulted snake skin: the owner remains recognisable in the garment. So clothing tells a story that reveals the vestiges and emotions of its owner.[2] In the study *Body Dressing*, Joanne Entwistle and Elizabeth Wilson call attention to this phenomenon from the perspective of fashion theory.[3] Clothing is concerned not only with an ideal look or the communication of identity; in our culture it also functions as an *embodied* practice: we are attached as persons to our clothing (and to that of our fellow human beings) and we form a relationship with it. Until quite recently, fashion designers rarely took these physical, tactile and intimate aspects of clothing into account in their design process. But in the past few decades, the experience and related narrative aspects of clothing have been explored in a number of ways.

In *Structural Mode* (2012) Rejina Pyo (South Korea) examines the ways in which colour and materials influence each other and what effect the choice of material has on the colour, volume and fall of a fabric. Almost like a painter, she focuses

Rejina Pyo,
Structural Mode,
spring/summer 2011

explicitly on the expression of the material itself. Jennifer Gadient (Switzerland) works more from a sculptor's perspective and bases her clothing on the forms and structures of air bubbles, foam and glass, whose brevity fascinates her, as well as on the volumes that these materials can assume. Both designers add a 'formal' narrative value to clothing and fabric by emphasising their aspects of form and experience.

Wang Lei (China) tells a different story. He imparts form and new meaning to materiality by developing his materials himself: He spins threads from newspaper in such a way that the political topics from the newspapers are invisibly incorporated. So even the tactile, material layer of clothing can be laden with meaning.

Iris van Herpen (the Netherlands) goes one step further and shows that the old-fashioned nineteenth-century construction process – weaving a fabric, making a pattern, cutting and sewing – can be modernised and replaced by 3D printing and other advanced technological processes. The *new construction* generates a new *materiality*, and with it the possibility of creating new meaning.

In her *Voltage* collection of 2013, for example, Van Herpen depicts 'lightning', which she transforms into a dress by means of 3D printing. She never could have done this with 'ordinary textile' and the traditional dressmaking process. More practical – as well as more revolutionary – is the *Wearable Solar* dress (2013) by Pauline van Dongen (the Netherlands), which has solar cells worked into it that can charge a cell phone.

Iris van Herpen,
Voltage, couture 2013

In *Trans-For-M-otion* (2010), Eunjeong Jeon (South Korea) reveals emotions by having the fabric of his clothing turn colour according to the emotion of the wearer.

These new and 'smart' outfits change both the way the wearer relates to his clothing and the meaning he communi-

Pauline van Dongen,
Wearable Solar, 2013

cates. Do we clothe ourselves with these *wearables* to show the outside world who we are? Or is it mainly because we're in communication with our own bodies and we're able to show off our body's gastrointestinal activity, temperature and biochemical processes? And what effect does Van Herpen's poetic visual language have on the popular fashion aesthetic of elegance and an ideal female image with a luxury lifestyle? In what universe does Iris van Herpen's woman live? This is how many designers are embarking on a fundamental exploration of what the clothing of the future can be.

1 This process began to develop in the 1930s when fashion photography was introduced in the fashion magazines. Roland Barthes describes this development in *Système de la mode*, published in 1967. The further medialisation brought about by television, but mainly by the emergence of the internet, has made both brand identification and photogenic quality all the more important.

2 Barbara Vinken, 'Fashion: Art of Dying, Art of Living', in: Jan Brand and José Teunissen (eds.), *Fashion and Imagination*, Arnhem 2009, p. 72-92.

3 Joanne Entwistle and Elizabeth Wilson, *Bodydressing*, New York 2001, pp. 33-34.

4 The term *embodied cultural practice* is often used in women's studies and cultural studies and refers to the fact that cultural values and meanings are reflected in, and therefore derive meaning from, the clothed body. See Thomas J. Csordas, *Embodiment and Experience: The Existential Ground of Culture and Self*, Cambridge 1994.

Maison Martin Margiela
Martin Margiela

1957

M

● Belgium

Martin Margiela (1957, Genk, Belgium) and his fashion house Maison Martin Margiela is regarded as the most important European exponent of deconstructivist fashion. Margiela studied at the Royal Academy of Fine Arts in Antwerp along with Walter Van Beirendonck, Ann Demeulemeester, Dries Van Noten, Dirk Van Saene, Dirk Bikkembergs and Marina Yee, who later became known as the Antwerp Six. Martin Margiela is also sometimes thought of as the seventh member of this group. All of them were taught by the influential fashion instructor Linda Loppa. In 2002, Renzo Rosso, the founder of Diesel, bought a controlling interest in Maison Martin Margiela. But prior to that – exactly when is unknown – Martin Margiela had already left his fashion house.

www.maisonmartinmargiela.com

Exhibition
— *Pattern for a long coat*
  autumn/winter 1997-1998
  Paper, wire, string, metal
  Collection Museum Boijmans
  Van Beuningen, Rotterdam

The designs that come from Maison Martin Margiela bear all the signs of the trade. Margiela's design process is an investigation of what clothing is, with the emphasis on its construction. This is translated into inflated proportions, clearly visible seams, linings and hems, garments deliberately left unfinished and the deconstruction of existing garments into new ones. To keep people's attention from being diverted from the clothing, Martin Margiela hid himself from the public and seldom or never gave interviews. For this reason, while Margiela was still in charge of his label his designs were presented by blindfolded models.

In his collection for autumn/winter 1997-1998, Martin Margiela revealed the various phases of the design process. The idea is that almost every design can be traced back to the original pattern, just like the patterns in the archives of a dressmaker. Margiela did this as a way of criticising the fetishising of luxury goods, an upcoming trend in the fashion world at that time. Almost the entire collection consists of old articles of clothing that were cut apart by Margiela and his team and made into something new. A Stockman mannequin was converted into a waistcoat, cocktail dresses from the fifties were transformed into new dresses, and old army socks were unravelled and made into sweaters (with the heels of the socks cleverly positioned over the breasts and the elbows). Martin Margiela also created two separate sleeves that could be attached to the Stockman waistcoat as well as to other garments by means of accompanying needles. Margiela also made a men's jacket out of Tyvek, a synthetic material, in which the seams are indicated on the design as they are on a sewing pattern.

Martin Margiela presented this collection to the public in a most unusual way. The invitation was printed on a map of Paris, one of those maps that are distributed everywhere for free. Many of the guests thought it was junk mail and threw the invitation away. On the day of the catwalk show, Margiela presented his collection at three locations and the show was accompanied by a brass band. At the last location, a former dancing school, the models didn't parade down a catwalk inside the building but through the streets around it, mingling with the public.

A   *Pattern for a coat,*
    autumn/winter 1997-1998.
    Photography: Marina Faust

Anrealage
Kunihiko Morinaga

1980

M

■ Japan

Kunihiko Morinaga (1980, Tokyo, Japan) graduated in 2003 from Waseda University and the Vantan Design Institute, both in Tokyo. That same year he launched his own label, Anrealage, and brought out his first collection in 2005. Since then he has presented two new collections a year. Morinaga's work has won several prizes, including the Grand Prix of the New York Gen Art Competition for young designers in 2005 and the Mainichi Fashion Grand Prix and the Shiseido Incentive Award in 2011.

www.anrealage.com

Exhibition
— *Bone*
   spring/summer 2013
   Two ensembles; various
   fabrics and laser-cut polyester,
   which is made fluorescent
   and illuminated by UV light

The clothing from the Japanese Anrealage label (a fusion of the words *a real*, *unreal* and *age*) seems quite familiar, but at the same time it's hypermodern. This has nothing to do with the forms and silhouettes that designer Kunihiko Morinaga creates, most of which are fairly classical and filled with historical elements, especially in the collections since 2011. What is so radically modern about Morinaga's work is mainly the explosive mix of colours, prints and patterns: unlikely combinations of colours and patterns that have never been seen before and that bear no reference to any other fashion or era. Most of them were made with the help of the latest digital production techniques such as UV printing and laser cutting, after which the patterns were placed on top of each other once again or linked together into a kind of patchwork.

In the collection *8 bit low resolution* from 2011 this results in mosaic-like patterns, the same patterns that emerge when a digital low-resolution photo is blown up to an enormous size and the colours disintegrate into a cloud of colourful little blocks. Morinaga uses the subsequent pattern as a print for tailored jackets, dresses, pants, blouses, tights and shoes, and even for three-dimensional forms such as eyeglasses and the heels of pumps. The colours and forms almost seem not to have been designed at all but generated by a technical process with no human interference. Or perhaps they come directly from outer space.

At least as spectacular is the *Bone* collection from 2013. Here Morinaga depicts the construction of clothing in a series of contemporary hoop skirts, but without the fabric. What remains is the cage construction,

A

executed in bright colours or even in colours that glow in the dark. It's not so strange, then, that Lady Gaga, one of the birds of paradise of the pop circuit, wore one of the dresses from this collection in a video clip.

The *Color* collection, also from 2013, in which Morinaga goes even further in this exploration of colour, is downright moving. There's nothing very spectacular about the classical dresses, jackets and pants suits, which are particularly well-cut. Until they change colour under the influence of UV lights and are slowly transformed into a dreamy mix of soft and bright pastels. The familiar silhouettes, combined with the latest techniques and unprecedented colour combinations, are extremely alienating. Suddenly you realise that the future of fashion has already begun.

B

A-B *Bone*, presentation of the collection, spring/summer 2013. Photography: Anrealage Co., Ltd

Boundless
Zhang Da

1967

M

● China

Fashion designer Zhang Da (1967, Xi'an, China) began the prêt-à-porter line Boundless (*Meibian* in Chinese) in 2005, working from his studio in Shanghai. In 1990 he earned his bachelor's degree in fashion design from the North-West Textile College in Xi'an. After graduating Zhang Da stayed on as a teacher at the North-West Textile College. In 1997 he won the Mittel Moda International Young Designer competition. In addition to working for Boundless, he has also been working for the label Shang Xia, an initiative of the Hermès Group, since 2008. The clothing and accessory label Shang Xia incorporates Chinese influences in a modern way. Zhang Da's work for Boundless was shown at the Victoria and Albert Museum in London in 2008 as part of the exhibition *China Design Now*.

Exhibition
— *Circle tee (O-shirt)*
    spring/summer 2004
— *Circle dress*
    spring/summer 2008
    Flat collection
    since spring/summer 2002
    Polyester (95%), lycra (5%)

A

With his clothing label Boundless, Zhang Da repudiates the fashion rules that require a designer to present a completely new collection at least twice a year. Instead he designs clothing that knows no season, developing small 'capsule collections' based on a specific concept. Zhang Da derives his inspiration for Boundless from Chinese philosophy and the Chinese way of making clothing. This results in minimalistic designs made in soft, natural materials such as silk, cotton and linen. For his designs Zhang Da uses a 'flat cut', a technique that is much in use in Southeast Asian clothing and that is clearly reflected in the *O-shirt*. Says Zhang Da: 'That is the Chinese way of thinking – you don't make the finished garment itself, you make the system to generate it; the thing is not fixed but naturally comes out of the environment that you create. In Europe you can use the draping technique to make the form – you shape it perfectly the way you want it – even when you take it off to hang it on the rack, the shape is still there. But for my clothes, if you take it off from the body, it becomes flat.'[1]

Zhang Da's vision of the body is also taken from his Chinese identity. While Western fashion designers have developed cutting and sewing techniques to accentuate the hips and breasts, Chinese designers – as well as Japanese – approach the body in a more reserved way. Zhang Da's designs show the contours of the body but keep it well-covered at the same time. This means that more is left to the imagination.

This confrontation between his Eastern design practice and the enormous popularity of Western fashion in China is a source of tremendous fascination for Zhang Da. China's enormous economic growth has led to a great demand for design products, but this demand mainly leans towards luxury Western fashion houses. Many Chinese designers wrestle with the problem of finding their own style; many of them are still working with a combination of different Western styles. But according to Da interest in local Chinese products is slowly developing, and his design practice is growing bit by bit.

1   See www.modeschina.com/post/46740980126/zhang-da

A-B *Circle dress*,
    Flat collection, 2008.
    Photography: Peng Yang Jun

This is a photograph of a garment printed with text. The readable fragments include:

ITEM'S Surface The DESIGN is to draw your attention to it. We want you to BUY it. To the buyers... as PLEASURE. A good BRIEF DESIGN is... and gives more pleasure. This... you to READ IT. But if you have a free MIND... NOW! because... we are attempting to do is to... on. Yet this is a DOUBLE BIND because if you... doing what we tell you, and if you read on you'll be doing what we've wanted all along. And the more you read... for this simple device of telling you exactly how... all design works. They're TRICKS and this is the worst TRICK of all... TRICK you, and if you've read this far then you're TRICKED but you wouldn't have known this unless I told you.

This writing is to help SELL the ITEM and encourage... We hope... pick it up. This is known... trying to pull... designed to get you to read... STOP READING.

...What we are really suggesting and... or not buy an ITEM... is a con because if you agree... which is the design. The con is a con.

The sculptures of Christoph Broich are an attempt to manipulate proportions and perspective in order to mislead the public and to play with their sense of space. Take his trompe l'oeil-like *An Outfit* (2002). Broich's work is an investigation of the history of the materials and movements in today's art world, which he then combines with references from pop culture, thus creating an entirely unique, idiosyncratic signature. Broich wants to stimulate the public to think about how they relate to the space they are occupying and how the work relates to the art and fashion world.

An Outfit was shown at the exhibition *Ptychoseis = Folds and Pleats: Drapery from Ancient Greek Dress to 21st-century Fashion* in 2004 in the Benaki Museum in Athens. It is part of the collection of the Mode-Museum in Antwerp. The work is a canvas that is printed on the front and the back. 'An outfit' is sewn to the front of the canvas with a text printed over that. Christoph Broich took his inspiration for the text from the British new wave band XTC and their LP *Go 2* from 1978. Written on the sleeve of the record is an indictment against the

consumption culture. Broich adapted the text to his own views for *An Outfit*: 'This is a COLLECTOR'S ITEM. This writing is the DESIGN upon the ITEM'S SURFACE. The DESIGN is to help SELL the ITEM. We hope to draw your attention to it and encourage you to pick it up. Then we want you to BUY it.' So *An Outfit* has to do with the techniques of seduction that are used in the fashion world to convince the consumer to buy something. 'Luring the victim', as Broich himself puts it.

Broich exposed the canvas and the outfit to high temperatures and pressures of various intensities. Because each material has its own properties and thicknesses so that it responds to heat and pressure differently, all the materials undergo different degrees of discolouration and shrinkage. The back of the canvas underwent only slight pressure, so the black colour printed on it is blurred and has turned green. The result is an X-ray like image. Thus Christoph Broich refers to our outer appearance and the way fashion functions as a façade to clothe the outside and to keep our deepest interior, our soul, hidden.

Christoph Broich

Christoph Broich (1966, Stadt Blankenberg, Germany) moved to Antwerp in 1990 to attend the Royal Academy of Fine Arts, from which he received his master's degree in 1994. In 1996 he launched his own clothing label, and in 2001 he opened a flagship store. In 2005 Christoph Broich founded the Red Fish Factory, a cross-over company whose goal is to organise events in the area of design, fashion and art. Since 2006 Broich has focused more on sculptures and installations than on clothing design. With the Red Fish Factory Christoph Broich organises the NU Fashion Festival and the BHART Art Festival, among others.

www.christophbroich.com
www.redfishfactory.com

Exhibition
— *An Outfit* (limited edition, 20 pieces)
2002
Polyester, microfiber, double tricot, pins, transfer print
170 × 103 cm

1966

M

● Germany

B

A   *An Outfit*, in the studio, 2002.
Photography: Christoph Broich/Red Fish Factory
B   *DT (Double Take)*, *Jimi's Shirt* and *Jimi's Underwear*, in the studio, 2005.
Photography: Christoph Broich/Red Fish Factory

Carole Collet

1969

F

● France

Carole Collet (1969, Louhans, France) studied textile design at the École supérieure des Arts Appliqués Duperré in Paris and then at the University of the Arts in London. Since 2010 she has been a reader at the Central Saint Martins College of Art and Design of the University of the Arts in London, where she is deputy director of the Textile Futures Research Centre. She also works as curator design and design researcher. Her work has been shown in the United Kingdom, Germany, France, the Netherlands, China and Japan.

**www.carolecollet.com
www.vimeo.com/52572656**

Exhibition
— *Biolace*
 2010-2012
 **Two framed photographs
 and animation video
 59.4 × 42 cm**

By 2050 the population of the world is fully expected to number about 9 billion. Given the limited amount of agricultural land, it's going to be an enormous challenge to supply all those people with adequate food and clothing, especially if it's to be done in an environmentally friendly manner. Biotechnology and genetic engineering are already commonly being used in agriculture and food production to create varieties that produce a higher yield, for instance, or are resistant to certain diseases. But this involves interfering with existing DNA structures and with existing plants and other organisms. In her project *Biolace*, however, designer, researcher and curator Carole Collet goes one step further. Collet brings textile design and synthetic biology together in her search for new products and new ways of producing food and textiles. In her work, the modification of existing, natural life forms gradually changes into the designing of artificial life forms that appear nowhere in nature – or into the redesigning of existing systems (read: plants) in order to fill roles that are the specific responsibility of human beings. Examples are the black strawberry (Fragaria Fusca Tenebris), a plant whose fruit contains more vitamin C and antioxidants than the ordinary variety and whose roots produce black lace that can be used in textiles. Or the factor 60 tomato

(Tomatum Lycopene Fabricae), which produces tomatoes with lycopene that protects us from UV radiation and also has protein-rich roots with a subtle bacon flavour. Or 'golden nanospinach', which is not only a high-quality food but also produces microbiological transistors for the electronics industry. In Collet's view, textile design and production for the future have absolutely nothing to do with colours, patterns and structures but with much larger concepts: with what we need as human beings, with sociopolitical issues, with sustainability and with the careful management of scarce natural resources.

For her work and way of thinking Carole Collet has coined the term 'biofacture'. Biofacture is a means of production in which products are made – or grown, to be exact – in an organic way, which is quite different from the traditional manufacturing we have known for so long. She and her students at the Textile Futures Research Centre conduct research on the functioning, production and application of textiles that stretch the traditional understanding of textile. 'Our students come out thinking differently,' says Collet. 'They have the most weird, juicy, flavoursome ideas. The merging of biology and nanotechnology opens up a new world where designers could well turn into alchemists.'

A *Basil No. 5 (Ocimum Basilicum Rosa), Biolace,* 2010-2012. Photography: © Carole Collet, Central Saint Martins, University of the Arts, London
B *Strawberry Noir (Fragaria Fusca Tenebris), Biolace,* 2010-2012. Photography: © Carole Collet, Central Saint Martins, University of the Arts, London

A

B

A

B

Fashion is all about innovation, but according to Pauline van Dongen the fashion industry at least renders that designation totally meaningless. For decades now, fashion has been produced in more or less the same way with more or less the same materials, although a great deal more would be possible by collaborating with programmers and engineers. But then you'd have to have an open mind, a broader outlook and a more expansive vision.

Van Dongen herself collaborated with Freedom of Creation, and in 2010 she was the first in the world to develop a fully 3D-printed shoe. Her purpose was not to beat everyone else to the punch or to invent a nifty gadget, but to utilise a technology by which forms could be created that could not be made in any other way, a technology that would allow for very low production runs without requiring a set minimum. Even in those early days she used new technology to make her designs better, as a means and not as an end. She's come a long way since then. Now she focuses her creative, inquisitive spirit on the actual integration of technology in the making of textile. Working with a multidisciplinary team, she developed *Wearable Solar* in 2013, an elegant coat and an equally stylish dress in which 48 and 72 solar cells are integrated respectively. The solar cells are hidden and can only be seen when a compartment of the coat or dress is folded open. The solar cells are joined together and can be connected to a smart phone by means of a little plug. When the wearer walks in the sun, the phone can be fully charged in about two hours. Van Dongen is convinced that as electronic components become smaller and smaller, more of the electronics will be integrated into our clothing. She also predicts that the barriers to keeping electronics close to the skin will be increasingly lowered. Mobile telephones, smart watches, Google Glass: who gives these things a thought anymore? Is there anyone still afraid of them?

A coat with built-in LED lights that make you more visible in the twilight and the dark is the result of her collaboration with Philips Research. Here, too, aesthetics and functionality are combined in an extraordinary way. A beautiful coat during the day, extra security at night. But Van Dongen's thinking and dreaming is taking her even further: to making more use of 3D printing, because it will allow us to make garments only when we really need them, thus requiring fewer raw materials. To developing a fibre that converts sunlight directly into electrical energy. To the garments that you might weave or knit from such a fibre. To...

Pauline van Dongen

Pauline van Dongen (1986, Amsterdam, the Netherlands) graduated from the ArtEZ Institute of the Arts in Arnhem in 2010. Her career got off to a flying start that same year with the 3D-printed shoe she developed with Freedom of Creation. In 2010 she also started her own womenswear label, combining new technologies with traditional craftsmanship. In March 2014 her *Wearable Solar* made it to the final round of *SXSW* Accelerator, the prestigious new technology festival that is held every year in Austin, Texas. Her designs have been shown on catwalks and exhibitions around the world and have received many awards. Pauline van Dongen is currently working on her doctorate at Eindhoven University of Technology.

www.paulinevandongen.nl

1986

F

● The Netherlands

Exhibition
— *Wearable Solar* dress
2013
Leather, wool, solar panels
90 × 50 cm
The multidisciplinary team of *Wearable Solar* comprises Pauline van Dongen, Christiaan Holland (project manager Gelderland Valoriseert) and Gert Jan Jongerden (solar energy expert)

A *Wearable Solar* jacket, 2013. Model: Julia J., Fresh Model Management. Photography: Mike Nicolaassen
B *Wearable Solar* dress, 2013. Model: Julia J., Fresh Model Management. Photography: Mike Nicolaassen

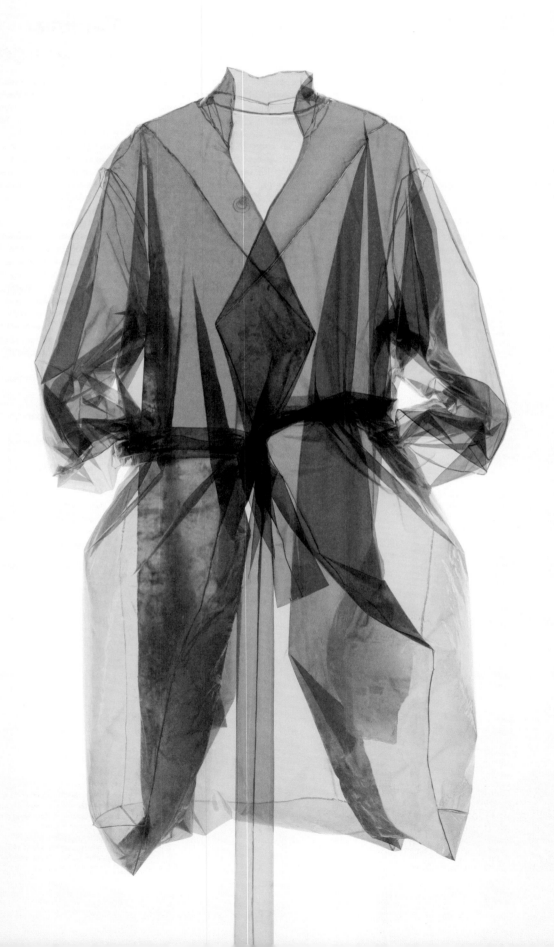

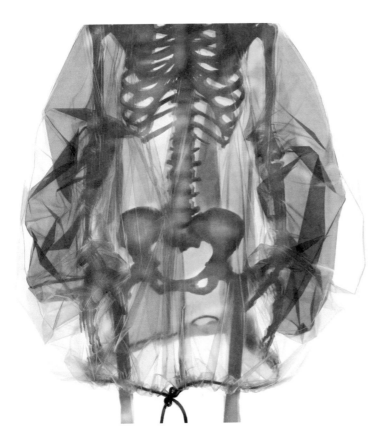

B

Jennifer Gadient

Jennifer Gadient (1988, Walen-stadt, Switzerland) earned her bachelor of arts diploma in 2012 from the Institute of Fashion Design in Basel. During and after her course of study Gadient worked as a costume designer for theatre, opera and ballet – something she still does in addition to her work as an independent fashion designer. Gadient tries to strike a balance with her designs between aliena-tion, attraction and rejection in order to arrive at an entirely per-sonal aesthetic. She wants to confront without causing shock. In 2009 Jennifer Gadient won the Triumph Inspiration Award for her undergarments, which were inspired by the shape of the hula hoop.

www.jennifergadient.com

1988

F

● Switzerland

<u>Exhibition</u>
— *Inflatable Smoky Coat*
   spring/summer 2012
   PVC film
   c. 105 × 75 × 45 cm

Jennifer Gadient's designs are mostly inspired by the forms and structures of air bubbles, foam and glass. She is fascinated by the transience of these materials as well by the volumes they are able to assume. This fascination is translated directly into her designs, which often take on an imposing form. Jennifer Gadient also likes looking at microscopic images of insects and bacteria, which reveal a layered world that is normally hidden from human eyes. Finally, the Swiss fashion designer finds inspiration in X-rays, which expose the hidden structures of the human body, something that is immediately reflected in her work. The silhouette of the body is always clearly visible in her designs because Gadient frequently works with transparent materials such as lightly-coloured PVC. If PVC is inflated with hot air and the parts are then fused together, the designs can be moulded; in this respect Gadient works more like a sculptor than a fashion designer. The *Inflatable Smoky Coat* comes from the *Plastic Poetry* collection for spring/summer 2012. In designing this coat, as well as the other PVC designs in this collection, Gadient did not work on the body directly. First she cut out large pieces of PVC, and only when these pieces were inflated did they begin conforming more to the body.

C

In this way the form of the body dictates the silhouette.

In addition to various PVC designs, the collection also contains oversized sweaters, dresses and coats made from soft materials such as silk and velour. Using these mater-ials, Jennifer Gadient conducts her research into fashion that protects the body and fashion that hides the body. By combining the soft materials with something unusual like PVC, she hopes to stimulate the public into developing their visual sensibilities and thinking about the conventions that are part of fashion.

A   *Inflatable Smoky Coat*,
    spring/summer 2012.
    Photography: Christian Schnur
B   *Pullover*, spring/summer 2012.
    Photography: Christian Schnur
C   Weldering of the inflatable parts,
    spring/summer 2012

A

Ying Gao

1973

F

● China

Ying Gao (1973, Beijing, China) studied fashion at the Haute école d'arts appliqués in Geneva and the Université du Québec in Montréal, Canada, where she earned her master's degree in multimedia. After graduation she worked in Paris, Montreal and Beijing, among other places, first as a trend fore-caster and later as a fashion de-signer and instructor. In her own projects she conducts research on new fabrics and interactive clothing. Gao has been a professor at the Université du Québec à Montréal since 2003 and has also been working as the head of de-sign in the fashion, accessories and jewellery department of the Haute école d'art et de design in Geneva since January 2014.

www.yinggao.ca

Exhibition
— *Incertitudes*
2013
Two interactive garments:
PVDF, dressmaker pins,
electronic devices
70 × 40 × 25 cm

In the eyes of Ying Gao, fashion can only have meaning if it is both radical and experi-mental. Gao began her professional career in the middle of the 1990s as a fashion designer, became interested in new tech-niques a few years later while studying for her master's degree in Multimedia, and since then has produced work on the cutting edge of avant-garde fashion and art. While normally the only relationship a garment forms is with the person who is wearing it, Gao attempts to trigger an interaction between the garment and the environment. In this she is mainly interested in non-material environmental factors such as light, air and sound.

It's an amusing game Gao is playing here, but with serious undertones. The individual is besieged by external factors and the garment functions as a protective layer.

In *(No)where (Now)here* (2013) Gao investigates the relationship between material and the intangible, that is, between the garment and the glance of the observer. The sensors implanted in the fabric of these dresses respond to the human glance and set off a number of tiny engines that make the fabric undulate; it's as though the dress were responding directly to being looked at. The idea of 'smart textiles' and 'intelligent clothing' immediately comes to mind, but Gao thinks that's nonsense: the intelligence

A

In the project *Playtime* (2011), which takes its name from the famous film by Jacques Tati, Gao designed two interactive dresses, dresses that seem to be wrapped up in their own very private and rather obstinate lives. Contrary to what is regarded as the highest ideal in the world today (and not only for fashion) – to have one's picture taken and distributed via the internet – the dresses refuse, as it were, to let themselves be photographed. One dress has sensors in the fabric that cause the garment to begin moving whenever a camera is aimed at it, thereby blurring the image. The other produces an enormous amount of light so that taking a good photo is impossible.

is exclusively the property of whoever made the garment in the first place.

In her most recent project, *Incertitudes* (2013), Gao introduced a large number of dressmaker pins into dresses made of white and silver fabric. The pins are connected to sensors and all sorts of other electronics, and they react to environmental sounds and the human voice. The dresses are – quite literally – conversation pieces. Despite the advanced technology that Gao uses, she's not really interested in the technology. She's searching for a dialogue between the garment and the observer, but a dialogue full of riddles and poetry such as the dis-creet tingling of the pins.

A-B *Incertitudes*, 2013.
Photography: Mathieu Fortin

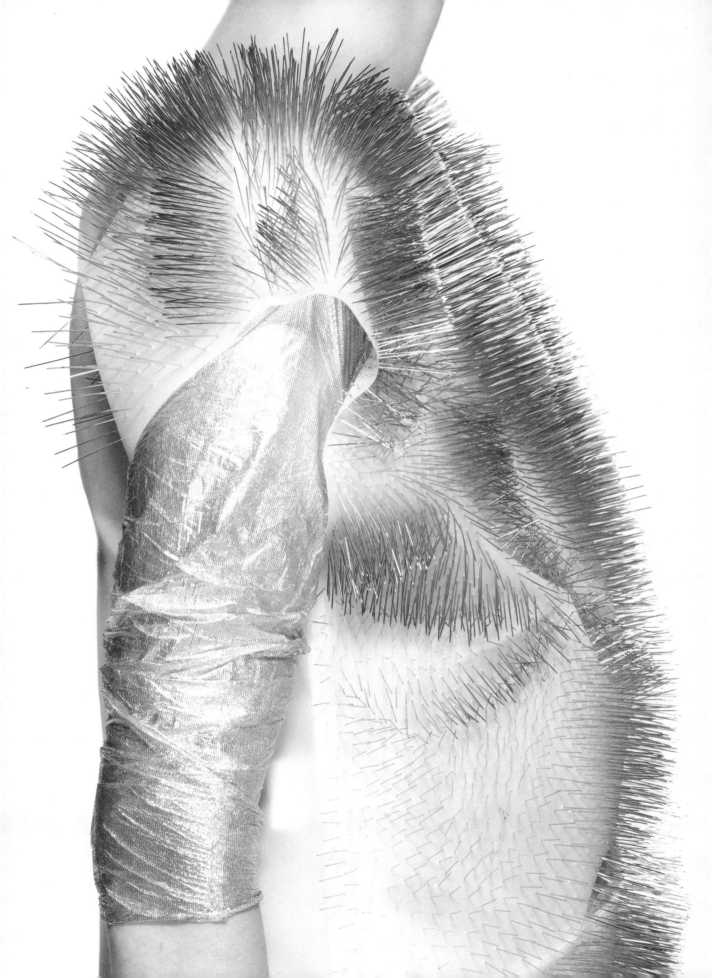

During the 1980s, Helen Storey was one of the 'angry young women' of the British fashion world. Her name was mentioned in one and the same breath with those of Vivienne Westwood, Katharine Hamnett and John Galliano, her often provocative clothing was worn by stars such as Cher and Madonna, she was voted the Most Innovative Designer and Best Designer Exporter in 1990 and, in that same year and the year that followed, she was nominated for British Designer of the Year. But even in the collections that made her famous, the love-hate relationship she had with fashion was hard to avoid. Evening dresses with bare bottoms, dresses imprinted with the image of a foetus or a company logo, and boas made from rags did more to cast doubt on the traditional view of women, glamour and luxury than to contribute to it. In the mid-nineties Storey closed the doors to her fashion house and turned her attention to a new field of research that combined several different disciplines such as art, biology, the neurosciences and chemistry.

The first result of her new life was *Primitive Streak*, a collection of twenty-seven fabrics and garments that are based on the first thousand hours of human existence, from fertilisation to the moment the human form becomes recognisable. She developed this collection with her sister Kate, a developmental biologist. In 1997 Storey and Caroline Coates founded the Helen Storey Foundation, a non-profit organisation based on creativity and innovation in which several different disciplines join forces to come up with answers to the big questions and problems of our age. Sustainability is one of the problems, so Storey and chemist Tony Ryan and a number of other partners developed a clothing collection that purifies air, calling it the *Catalytic Clothing* project. She also worked with Ryan on *Dissolving Bottles* and *Disappearing Dresses*. The plastic bottles dissolve in hot water and form a gel that can serve as a substrate for seeds. The dresses also dissolve when hung in a large fish bowl filled with water, creating spectacular underwater fireworks. It's not just an aesthetic image, connected to the aesthetics of fashion, it's much more than that. For Storey and Ryan it's also a metaphor. A dress that took months to create disappears in a couple of days, just as the world will do if we aren't careful and continue with our present way of life and production. The *Disappearing Dresses*, with their vanishing beauty, should alert us to the unfathomable depth of that loss.

Helen Storey Foundation
Helen Storey

1959

F

■ United Kingdom

Helen Storey (1959, London, United Kingdom) studied fashion at Kingston University in London and did an internship in Rome with Valentino and Lancetti. Back in London she launched her own label in 1983 and quickly made a name for herself during the post-punk era with her provocative designs that flawlessly reflected the spirit of the times. But she had had enough of the fashion world, and in 1995 she published an autobiography with the telling title *Fighting Fashion*. In the mid-nineties she turned to collaborating with scientists from various disciplines, conducting research on clothing and textiles and on the way they influence the environment. Storey is a Senior Research Fellow and Professor of Fashion and Science at the London College of Fashion, and she has received honorary doctorates from several universities.

www.helenstoreyfoundation.org

Exhibition
— *Say Goodbye*
  2010
  Installation, polyvinyl alcohol, *Disappearing Dresses* (since 2008)
  In collaboration with Trish Belford (textiles) and professor Tony Ryan OBE (scientist)

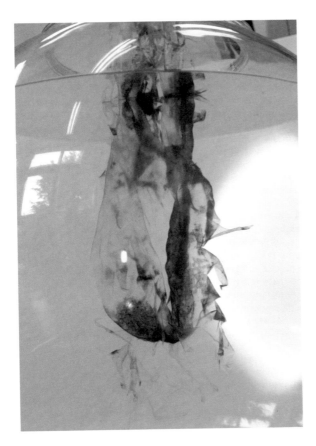

A   *Say Goodbye*, installation, 2010.
Photography: Francis Ware,
© Royal Academy of Arts, London
B   *Wonderland*, early experiment with dissolvable textile, 2006.
Photography: Trish Belford

A

B

Pia Interlandi

1985

F

■ Australia

Pia Interlandi (1985, Melbourne, Australia) studied fashion and design at RMIT University in Melbourne and held an internship with the Japanese designers Masahiro Nakagawa and Yoshiki Hishinuma. In 2006 she graduated cum laude, and one year later she began her own label with Priscilla Lim, Hhhh..., which should be pronounced as a brief sigh. Since 2011 she has turned her full attention to clothes for the dying and the dead, and in 2012 she began her own *Garments for the Grave* practice. She also works as an instructor and mentor at RMIT University, where she earned her doctorate in 2013, and she is regularly asked to give lectures on clothing and death.

www.piainterlandi.com

Exhibition
— *Tailored Jacket*
   (4 garments)
   2011
   Dissolvable fabric

A

A   *Bodysuit*, 2001.
   Photography: Devika Bilimoria
B   *Tailored Jacket*, 2011.
   Photography: Devika Bilimoria

In our modern age, where everything seems to revolve around eternal youth, death is often painstakingly suppressed and almost completely outlawed, as if it didn't exist and wasn't part of life. In the fashion world, too, the focus is on youth, power and beauty, and mortality seems like a totally foreign concept. In the work of the Australian designer Pia Interlandi, however, mortality is the operating principle. Even in her early years at university she did research on the impermanence of fabrics and clothing, which she saw as a metaphor for the impermanence of life itself. For her research she cut garments into pieces as if performing an autopsy, or used materials that are highly perishable. When her grandfather died in 2008 and she was given permission to dress him for the funeral, her work took on another dimension. The big, powerful, proud man she had known had disappeared during the last months of his life, and it touched Interlandi deeply that she was able to evoke all that with the last clothing he would ever wear. From that moment on she began to concentrate entirely on clothing and the rituals surrounding death and burial.

In *The Pig Project* she conducted research using twenty-one dead pigs from the meat industry. The pigs were washed and embalmed with natural oils, then buried in biodegradable materials. After different periods of time the pigs were dug up to see how much the carcasses and materials had decayed. Or rather, to see to what extent they had entered into the endless cycle of life and death.

In 2012 Interlandi began her *Garments for the Grave* practice. In consultation with surviving relatives she creates tailor-made clothing for the deceased. The clothing is always made from highly biodegradable materials to keep from hindering the disintegration of the body and to allow the mortal remains to quickly return to the earth. It wasn't long, however, before her focus shifted from the dead to people in their last stage of life, and now she designs the last garments they will ever wear. Clothing is our second skin, says Interlandi — an important part of ourselves. By reflecting on what we're going to wear when we are buried, we begin an essential conversation about our own lives.

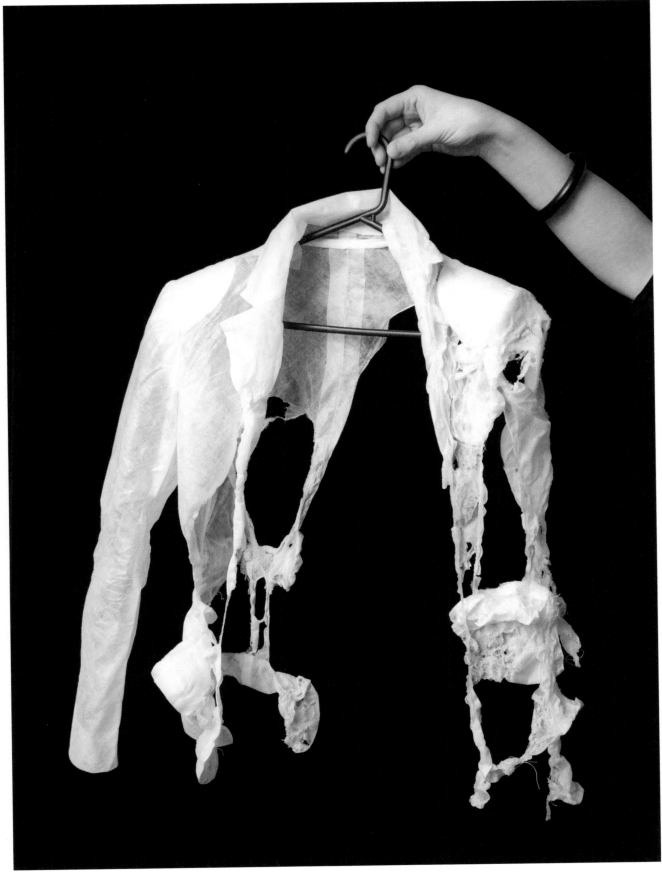

B

Protection has traditionally been one of clothing's most important functions, and it is this very function that Eunjeong Jeon, a designer of Korean origin, has been investigating, analysing and enlarging on in her work. Jeon conducted conversations with many women about their experiences of the so-called 'transitional spaces' you pass through between interior and exterior spaces, such as airports, train and metro stations and shopping centres, but sometimes simply out in the street. Places where sudden changes can occur in temperature, sound levels, pollution and the amount of clutter, but also in terms of crowds and even criminality. Many of the women admitted to feeling insecure or anxious in such spaces, by which they were also saying that in such places and at such moments their clothing did not provide adequate protection.

In her project *Trans-For-M-otion* (2010), Jeon develops experimental fabrics and clothing that respond directly to a changing environment. She uses wool as a basic material into which she incorporates all sorts of technical elements such as sensors, air-absorbing cells and LED lights. While 'ordinary' fabrics and garments only 'give' with the movements of the body, the sensors in Jeon's garments immediately signal how the wearer is feeling in a particular environment. Heartbeat, body temperature, respiration, muscle tension – all this is registered and processed. When the person feels anxious or insecure, for example, small cells in the garment fill up with air like little cushions so that the garment immediately fits closer to the body. The wearer is protected, as it were, and will begin to feel safer. The LED lights also respond directly to the wearer's movements and emotion. In the work shown at Museum Boijmans Van Beuningen, the wearer herself can also intervene. By pulling the garment up higher, a large, protective collar is formed that hides part of the face and functions as a mask.

Jeon herself sees her design as an interactive instrument that can be handled playfully and can be a source of great fun, as her research clearly reveals. To her surprise, the women in the interviews first spoke about the protective function of clothing during moments of insecurity, but after putting on the test models they happily gave in to manipulating and controlling the clothing with their bodies.[1] Research on so-called 'smart textiles' has only just begun, but it's certain to bring about a fundamental change in the way we relate to the clothes we wear.

1   Bradley Quinn, *Fashion Futures*, London 2012, pp. 222-231.

Eunjeong Jeon

Eunjeong Jeon (1970, Seoul, South Korea) conducts research on the relationships between clothing, emotions and the environment. She studied at the Danish Institute for Study Abroad in Copenhagen and in 1997 graduated with a degree in sculpture from the School of Fine Arts of Hongik University in Seoul. She then worked for a number of years as a furniture designer before moving to Australia. In 2005 she took a master's degree in Design in Art Furniture and Emotional Design from Curtin University of Technology in Perth, from which she also earned her doctorate in 2013. Since 2013 she has been working as a post-doctoral researcher in Industrial Design at Eindhoven University of Technology.

Exhibition
— *Trans-For-M-otion (II):*
   Disguise Garment
   2010
   Wool felt, LEDs
   120 × 85 × 0.32 cm

1970

F

● South Korea

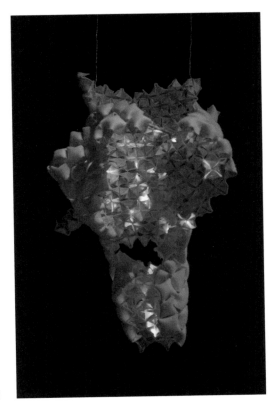

B

A   *Trans-For-M-otion (IV):*
    Touch me, Feel me,
    Play with me, 2010.
    Photography: Kyunghoon Kim
B   *Trans-For-M-otion (II):*
    Disguise Garment, 2010.
    Photography: Eunjeong Jeon

Mason Jung uses his designs to expose the many conventions that are prevalent in the fashion world, conventions having to do with the construction of a garment, the context in which the garment is shown and how it is worn. 'My inspiration is based on the antipathy towards formal wear for its fossilised forms and attributes of restricting individuality.'[1] Jung's design process is guided by the four C's: conception, construction, communication and consumption.

In the exhibition *The Future of Fashion is Now*, Mason Jung's *Sleeping Suit* (2009) is on display. Jung's inspiration for *Sleeping Suit* came from his two-year stint in the Korean army, where sleeping bags and blankets were standard issue. This fact, and the strict rules that apply in the army,

gave Mason Jung the idea of creating a new form for the men's suit, which is also a formal piece of equipment that is tied up with conventions. His guiding principle here was the concept of 'transformation'. Another key concept in Jung's design process in addition to 'transformation' is 'individuality'.

There's little room for individuality in the traditional men's suit; according to Jung it exudes controlled behaviour. Jung's *Sleeping Suit* is made from archetypical men's suit materials, such as wool and cotton. In order to emphasise the restrictive and controlling character of the suit, Mason Jung presents it on an enormous clothes hanger. It's his playful and unconventional manner of searching for ways to reinvent the men's suit while endeavouring to keep it wearable. This way of

Mason Jung

Mason Jung (1977, Seoul, South Korea) began his career in South Korea, where he received his bachelor's degree in Clothing and Textiles from Kyung Hee University, then went on to work for various fashion labels. In 2007 he moved to London to continue his studies at the Royal College of Art. For his graduation collection in 2009 – and for the work that followed – he found inspiration in his Korean roots. Jung is interested in restriction, rules, discipline and the way ideologies make themselves known in daily life. After graduation, Mason Jung began working at Maison Martin Margiela before starting his own label. In 2009 he won the prize for Fashion Collection of the Year at ITS#8 (International Talent Support).

www.masonjung.com

Exhibition
— *Sleeping Suit*
— *Blanket Suit*
   2009
   Wool

1977

M

● South Korea

A

working can also be seen in his *Camouflage Series* from 2010. The starting point for this collection was once again the classical men's wardrobe, which Jung redesigned with a strong sense of humour and a subtle hand. The *Camouflage Shirt*, for example, is a cross between a dress shirt and an overcoat. Outwardly it looks like two different garments while actually it's only one.

1   See www.rca.ac.uk/showcase/show-rca/mason-jung/

A   Putting on *Sleeping Suit*,
       2009

Julia Krantz

1982

F

■ Sweden

Julia Krantz (1982, Göteborg, Sweden) graduated from the Högskolan för Design och Konsthantverk in Göteborg in 2010. It took a while for her to find her place: Krantz had made earlier attempts at studying media and communication sciences, political science and film studies. With her graduation collection *Shell* she attracted the attention of many leading design magazines. After graduating Julia Krantz launched her own label, which straddles the line between fashion and autonomous art. Central to Krantz's work is her desire to create a fashion for the future.

www.juliakrantz.com

Exhibition
— *Shell* collection
   (1 garment)
   2009
   Silk, cotton, steel
   115 × 65 × 40 cm

In Julia Krantz's graduation collection *Shell* (2009) the dominating theme is structures. The collection shows transparent fabrics draped over metal frames that are inspired by the human anatomy, the body's organs and its symmetries, as well as by everything humans use to protect and decorate their bodies. Krantz has constructed something like a second skeleton around the female body, which first follows the lines of the body but then goes off on its own route, creating new forms. Instead of making initial sketches on paper, Julia Krantz works directly on the body with the metal and fabrics she has chosen. Because the fabrics are transparent and therefore allow light to pass through, a new three-dimensional experience around the body is created. The new forms and volumes radiate power, says Krantz, and in this way they prepare the wearer for the future.

This future is also featured in other designs by Julia Krantz. With her *Whiteness* collection from 2011 Krantz's aim was to design clothing for a futuristic female warrior: '*Whiteness* celebrates magnificent people in times of popular uprisings and digital revolutions.' Julia Krantz didn't just design clothing for *Whiteness* but she also told her story with photographs and graphic design. She used texts from insurgents who took part in the Egyptian revolution of 2011 and Wikipedia entries about important revolutionary moments in history.

This social awareness can also be found in the project *Cross-Bearer*, which Julia Krantz developed with photographer and art director Garri Frischer in 2011. In *Cross-Bearer* the focus is on self-realisation, something that is regarded as a major good in society today. This work is Krantz's criticism of this desire. 'Through lack of ideals we worship constructed identities as contemporary icons,' she says. Krantz believes that this obsessive desire has assumed almost religious forms and isolates us from the rest of society.

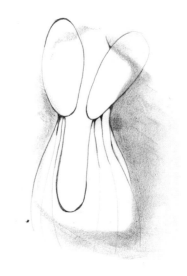

A

B

C

A   *Shell* collection, sketch, 2009
B   *Shell* collection, 2009.
    Photography: Julia Krantz
C   *Whiteness*, 2011.
    Photography: Garri Frischer
D   *Shell* collection, 2009.
    Photography: Katrin Kirojood

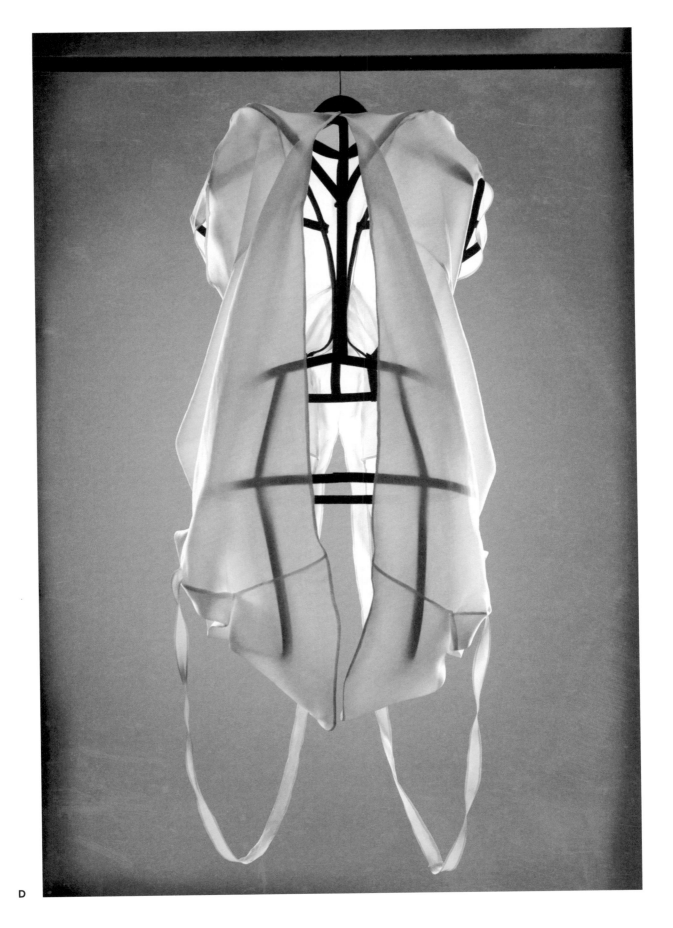

D

51

Victoria Ledig

1985

F

● Lithuania

Victoria Ledig (1985, Ventos, Lithuania) grew up in Berlin, where from 2005 to 2008 she studied to be a furniture maker. This is where her interest in 'real' materials and craftsmanship was born. She went on to study at the Design Academy Eindhoven, where she concentrated on material use but also experimented with many other facets of the design world. Her graduation project *Precious Skin* was nominated for the Melkweg Prize in 2013. Since 2011 Victoria Ledig has been part of the *Atelierdorp Eindhoven* design collective.

www.victorialedig.com

Exhibition
— *Precious Skin*
   2012
   Vegetable-tanned European calf leather, uncoated
   Tail bag: 50 × 33 × 18 cm
   Face clutch: 36 × 24 × 15 cm
   Leg etui: 23 × 8 × 4 cm
   Ear purse: 17 × 6 × 6 cm

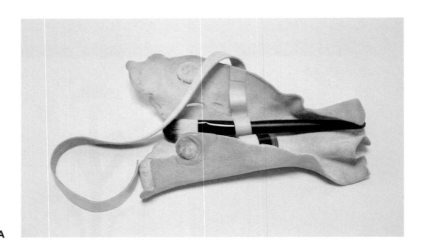

A

B

A   *Precious Skin* collection,
    leg etui, 2012.
    Photography: Victoria Ledig
B   *Precious Skin* collection,
    tail bag, 2012.
    Photography: Victoria Ledig
C   *Precious Skin* collection,
    ear purse, 2012.
    Photography: Victoria Ledig
D   *Precious Skin* collection, 2012.
    Photography: Victoria Ledig

Just as most consumers don't know (or don't want to know) where their pork chop comes from, so most fashion lovers have little or no awareness of the relationship between the fine leather from which their shoes and bags are made and the animals that provide the leather. For Victoria Ledig, however, that relationship is patently obvious and is the main idea behind her graduation collection *Precious Skin*.

While studying at the Design Academy Eindhoven she did an internship at the ECCO tannery in Dongen and became fascinated by leather as a material and by its many applications. But she was very aware of the relationship between the living hide of an animal and leather as a product: 'Leather is not a flat, sterile material. It once ran in the fields. It had wrinkles and folds. It's very beautiful, the real hide of a cow.'[1] In the tannery she also learned that only the hide from a cow's trunk is used to be made into leather. She was curious about what happened to the rest of the hide, so she visited an abattoir. To the surprise and even the dismay of the employees there she said she wanted to take the parts that were never used and have them tanned into leather. It was impossible, she was warned, to make leather from the ears, tails, heads and the lower parts of the leg. But that wasn't true. Even these parts could be used to make beautiful, very soft and naturally tanned leather. Ledig decided not to hide the origin of the leather but rather to emphasise it. In her collection of bags and cases, the head and legs of the calf can easily be recognised. By keeping the stitching and other finishing touches to a minimum, she is able to stay very close to the original material so that the living animal is almost shining through. In the publicity photos of the project, the relationship between hide and leather is subtly but inescapably depicted. The white skin of the chaste naked model combines almost effortlessly with the soft leather of the bags. A bag can't get any closer to our naked selves than that.

1   See www.we-heart.com/2013/11/22/victoria-ledig-precious-skin

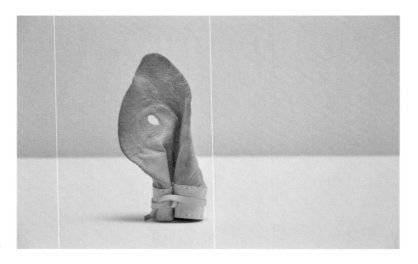

C

A

B

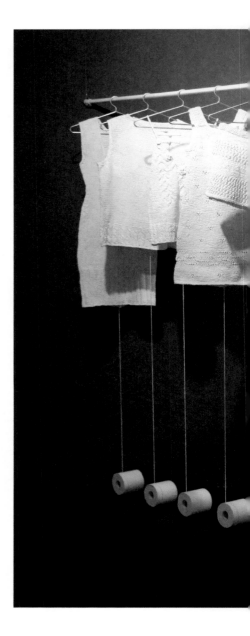

C

The artist Wang Lei does not work with fabric at all but with various kinds of paper. He spins thread from it, which he then knits, braids or weaves in order to make clothing from it. His interest in materials emerged during his years of study at the Central Academy of Fine Arts in Beijing. While taking a course in Expression of Material Language, Lei realized that as a farm boy the most logical thing for him was to start working with material that was cheap and within reach: toilet paper. He conducted extensive research on the properties of toilet paper and finally decided to dampen it and to turn them into twisted threads. He then knitted traditional Chinese clothing from the thread so that his work remains comprehensible for the observer despite the unusual material. Says Wang Lei: 'When I began studying the properties

Wang Lei

Wang Lei (1980, Henan, China) grew up in the Chinese country-side, the middle child in a family of five. His sister, who was eight years older than Lei, took care of him when he was young and taught him to knit and weave. Wang Lei wasn't immediately interested in fashion. He first studied drama. During that time he developed a love for theatrical costumes, which interested him more and more. In 2007 Wang Lei earned his master's degree in Experimental Art from the Central Academy of Fine Arts in Beijing.

1980

M

● China

Exhibition
— *Hand-Woven Toilet Paper*
   Since 2010
   Woven and twisted toilet paper

of the material I decided to make twisted thread from it, which I wove as part of my experimental exploration. From this I made a number of ordinary garments. This familiar language made the work more comprehensible, while the surprising process of turning paper into thread got the public thinking and stimulated their sense of discovery.' This resulted in the installation *Hand-Woven Toilet Paper* (since 2010). The installation consists of a series of garments knitted from toilet paper which hang from a frame as they would in a closet. The rolls of toilet paper are still connected to the bottom of the designs.

Wang Lei's work isn't just about materiality. It also contains socio-political overtones. He now uses other sources for his threads, including newspaper and paper from dictionaries and Bibles. *Fabrication No. 3*

from 2009, for example, is knitted from paper taken from a Chinese-English dictionary and created into two 'dragon' gowns such as those worn during the Qing Dynasty by the emperors and other members of the elite. Lei thus links the infallibility of these dignitaries with the infallibility of the dictionary, which always speaks the truth. The use of the dictionary – whose jacket was exhibited along with the dresses – refers to the running struggle for world domination between China and the West, according to Wang Lei.

A *Hand-Woven Toilet Paper*,
   National Art Museum of China,
   2013
B *Cultural China – Qing Dynasty*,
   2014, woven and twisted
   dictionary paper (Ci Hai). Private
   collection, Australia
C *Hand-Woven Toilet Paper
   No. 4*, 2010.
   Photography: Yang Haifeng

■ Japan   M + F   1973

mintdesigns
Hokuto Katsui and Nao Yagi

Mintdesigns was founded in 2001 by Hokuto Katsui (1973, Tokyo, Japan) and Nao Yagi (1973, Osaka, Japan). Katsui studied fashion at Parsons The New School for Design in New York and Yagi studied art criticism at Doshisha University in Kyoto. The two met when they were studying at Central Saint Martins College of Art and Design in London. After completing their studies there they returned to Tokyo to launch mintdesigns. Besides ladies' clothing the duo also makes children's clothes. Both are currently teaching in the Art & Design faculty of Osaka Seikei University.

www.mint-designs.com

Exhibition
— *Dazzling Puzzling*
autumn/winter 2013-2014
Garments and projections

The mintdesigns fashion label, which is the work of the Japanese duo Hokuto Katsui and Nao Yagi, has set its sights on making cheerful clothing that emphasises the expression of emotions. This is especially evident in the details of their designs, with the references to the duo's childhood days that are incorporated into them, and in the exuberant graphic prints they use. In their design process they allow themselves to be led by 'happy mistakes': mistakes or accidents that occur during designing that have an unexpectedly positive outcome. The duo see their designs as timeless products

A

B

that can enrich the daily lives of their wearers. The word 'mint' in mintdesigns refers to two things: the first is the idea of 'freshness' and the second suggests 'new' as in the expression 'in mint condition'.

Their collection *Dazzling Puzzling* for the autumn/winter of 2013-2014 is an overwhelming puzzle of shapes, colours and textures and was presented as such during Tokyo Fashion Week in March 2013. The décor design of the catwalk was in the hands of Yutaka Endo from the Luftzug Co designing agency: a large white wall was placed in the middle of the catwalk and ran down its entire length, so that the public on either side viewed the clothing against a white background. A large white grid of light was projected onto both sides of the catwalk, providing the designs with extra stratification – and this on top of the grids that had already been worked into many of the designs as prints or textures.

This method of presentation was adopted for the exhibition *The Future of Fashion*

is Now. Three outfits from the collection *Dazzling Puzzling* are shown in combination with a light projection. They reveal a simple, sporty silhouette, and the emphasis of the clothing is on comfort. The clear-cut lines of the designs accentuate the playful textures, colours and prints that Katsui and Yagi have given them and make the designs especially wearable, something that the duo aims for in all their clothing.

A-C Presentation of *Fashion Surgery
(a new hope)*, autumn/winter
2011-2012. Photography:
Yoshitsugu Enomoto
B   Presentation of *Dazzling Puzzling*,
autumn/winter 2013-2014.
Photography: Yoshitsugu
Enomoto

No religion is as theatrical as Catholicism, and in Latin America and Southern Europe in particular it's often a guaranteed source of baroque extravagance. As a young child Jef Montes had a lot of exposure to this kind of Catholicism thanks to his Spanish mother, and it clearly inspired his first collections: his graduation collection *Dolores* from 2012 for the ArtEZ Institute of the Arts and the *Illuminosa* collection from 2014. You can see it in the wide garments, for example, which fall in great pleats around the body and recall the images of the saints that are there to admire in every church or cathedral in Spain. But it's also apparent in the matching hats that encircle the models' heads like haloes, thereby referring to Catholic visual culture. The Communion candle was also a source of inspiration for Jef Montes's *Illuminosa*. During the presentation on the catwalk, the melting wax of the candles was represented by the blue ink that the model poured from two candle-like cylinders over her virginal white dress. Blue and white, two colours that have long been associated with Mary, were thus joined, creating a whimsical print and a provocative wet look – a surprising interpretation of a serene design.

The interesting thing about Montes is that he has translated classical Catholic visual language in modern terms and has done it in a radical way. In fact, he often gives you the feeling that you're looking at the clothing of the future. To a great extent this is owing to the high-tech materials he uses. Often these are developed by Montes himself from things that are readily available at any home improvement centre. Fire-resistant UD glass fibre, for example, is combined with wool, silk, felt, satin duchesse or viscose and steamed or treated with fire. Glass textiles are processed with chemically manipulated pigments, fabrics are reinforced with layers of silicon wax or nylon netting twine, and skirts and jackets are fastened by magnets. Cheap basic materials are thus worked and transformed in all sorts of ways and are given what might be called the haute couture treatment. The haute couture idea is intensified by the use of artisanal techniques such as draping, embroidery and hand-colouring. It's not surprising, then, that a garment by Montes often takes a week to produce. But he also makes creations that are highly wearable and exceptionally elegant.

Jef Montes

Jef Montes (1987, Arnhem, the Netherlands) received his bachelor's degree from the ArtEZ Institute of the Arts in Arnhem in 2012. After having presented his graduation collection *Dolores* as a member of the Class of 2012 during Amsterdam Fashion week he began a label under his own name. His first collection was presented during the 2014 Mercedes Benz Amsterdam Fashion Week. Jef Montes lives and works in Arnhem.

www.jefmontes.com

<u>Exhibition</u>
— *Illuminosa* collection
   2014
   Fibreglass, wool and
   embroidery, treated with
   flame, water and steam
— *Velero*-collection
   (1 garment)
   2015
— *De Profundis*
   2014
   Video: Koen Hauser
   in collaboration with
   Maarten Spruyt

B

C

A   *Illuminosa*, beret and coat, 2014
B   *Illuminosa*, 2014. Model: Vera
    Luijendijk, Paparazzi Model
    Management. Photography:
    Sabrina Bongiovanni,
    Solar Initiative
C   *Illuminosa*, detail, 2014

Jum Nakao

1966

M

■ Brazil

Jum Nakao (1966, São Paulo, Brazil) is a Brazilian fashion designer and creative director with Japanese ancestors. He studied art at the Fundação Armando Alvares Penteado and costume history at the Instituto Iberoamericano de Museología in São Paulo. He has worked as a style director for Zoomp, one of the biggest fashion companies in Brazil, and designed a premium line for Nike. He has also designed clothing for the Brazilian tennis star Gustavo Kuerten, and in 2012 he designed the costumes for the closing ceremony of the London Olympic Games and the Paralympics. Jum Nakao's work has been exhibited in Brazil, France, United Kingdom and New Zealand, among other places.

www.jumnakao.com

Exhibition
— *A Costura do Invisível
   – Sewing the Invisible*
   spring/summer 2004
   Dress made of vegetable paper
   and performance/show video
   90 × 90 × 200 cm

A

A-B *A Costura do Invisível
   – Sewing the Invisible*,
   performance/show, 2004.
   Photography: Fernando Louza

It was with a mixture of horror, disbelief and at first even a bit of indignation that the public watched the end of the show *A Costura do Invisível* by the Brazilian designer Jum Nakao at the Museu Oscar Niemeyer in Curitiba in Brazil. For four minutes they witnessed a poetic, almost magical parade of the most delicate designs they had ever seen, and now all that beauty was being torn from the bodies of the models – by the models themselves – and thrown to the floor. For four minutes the models had strutted down the catwalk dressed from head to toe in black cat suits that covered them completely, including their hands and feet, with the white paper constructions – the objects of the show – standing out beautifully against all that black. Because that's what it was all about: paper fashion. Nakao had used laser cutting machines to cut the most fantastic patterns out of paper, some

of which resembled lace or filigree. Reliefs had also been applied to some of the garments, and sometimes the paper was folded into origami-like constructions in order to provide volume. Crinolines were used to create volume as well, resulting in Victorian silhouettes that, unlike the hoop skirts of olden days, were light, frivolous and transparent.

Seven hundred hours of work and almost a ton of paper had gone into these designs, and in a couple of minutes it was all gone. What Jum Nakao wanted to show – the idea behind the project – was that material doesn't matter in the fashion world: 'People today think that everything has to be made in high definition, or in gold or silk, but none of that is of any importance. Sometimes we have to reflect on our values once again, on what it's really all about.'

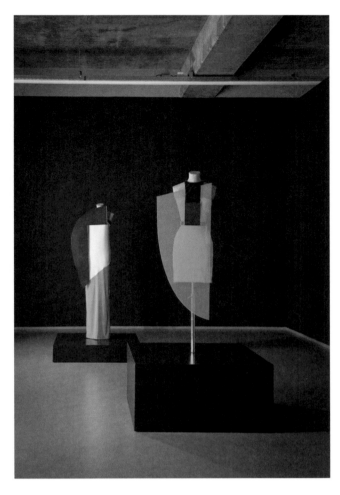

B

Rejina Pyo

Rejina Pyo (1983, Seoul, South Korea) earned her master's degree in Womenswear in 2011 from Central Saint Martins in London. A few of the pieces from her graduation collection were shown in the exhibition *Arrrgh! Monsters in Fashion* at the Benaki Museum in Athens. After graduating, Rejina Pyo began working as an assistant designer for Roksanda Ilincic's label. She also continued working on her own projects. She designed a collection for the Swedish high-street label Weekday as well as collections for her own label. In 2012 Pyo won the Han Nefkens Fashion Award and presented her work *Structural Mode* at Museum Boijmans Van Beuningen.

www.rejinapyo.com

Exhibition
— *Structural Mode*
(2 dresses)
spring/summer 2011
Mixed media, textiles,
perspex, aluminium
c. 134 × 70 × 36 cm
Collection Museum Boijmans
Van Beuningen, Rotterdam,
loaned by Han Nefkens Fashion
on the Edge, 2012

1983 F ● South Korea

Rejina Pyo won the Han Nefkens Fashion Award in 2012. An amount of 25,000 euros was attached to the prize, 15,000 euros of which was intended to finance the making of an exhibition. Pyo used the money to create *Structural Mode*, which was exhibited in the autumn of 2012 in the Willem van der Vorm Gallery and the Serra Gallery of Museum Boijmans Van Beuningen in Rotterdam. Her work consisted of sculptural dresses executed in a bright colour palette and with materials such as plexiglas and metal, which rotate around the body in spirals, curves and circles. Rejina Pyo's aim with these designs is to examine the relationship between wearable fashion and sculptural art. Pyo: 'The boundary between art and fashion is always somewhat blurred, so I wanted to experiment with a more direct approach. Instead of creating garments inspired by the colour, mood or design of an art piece, I wanted to create sculptural art that had been influenced by garments. None of the pieces are wearable, although at first glance they look like dresses or garments to some degree. Up close however, you can see the pieces are made using metal and plastics along with fabric, becoming sculptures in their own right.'[1]

In *Structural Mode* Rejina Pyo elaborated on the concept of her graduation collection from Central Saint Martins in London. She also took inspiration from the work of minimal artist Ellsworth Kelly, with his simple aesthetic and geometric colour fields. His abstract paintings from the 1950s made an especially deep impression on Pyo and found their way to the designs of her graduation collection. This consisted of floor-length dresses in primary colours, combined with sturdy wooden sculptures that the models carried with them on the catwalk. Rejina Pyo's inspiration for these sculptures, which bear some resemblance to totem poles, came from the work of the Japanese-American sculptor Isamu Noguchi. Assisted by the Korean sculptor Jaehyo Lee, Pyo worked the wooden forms with a burner. The result was impressive: Pyo's wooden sculptures turned the models into avant-garde shamans making their way to a ritual ceremony.

1   See www.somamagazine.com/regina-pyo/

A-B Exhibition *Structural Mode*
at Museum Boijmans
Van Beuningen in 2012.
Photography: Lotte Stekelenburg

Sruli Recht

Sruli Recht (1979, Jerusalem, Israel) was born in Israel but grew up in Melbourne, Australia, where he graduated from the Royal Melbourne Institute of Technology with a degree in fashion design. In 2005 he moved to London. He worked for three seasons with Alexander McQueen, where he cut patterns and made showpieces for the catwalk. At the moment Recht is working from his studio/workplace/small-scale factory The Armoury in Reykjavik. In 2012 he opened his first shop there.

www.srulirecht.com

1979

M

● Israel

On YouTube there's a short film about four minutes long – not recommended for sensitive souls – in which a plastic surgeon removes a strip of skin measuring 11 by 1 centimetres from the abdomen of fashion and industrial designer Sruli Recht. Recht regarded the operation as a performance worth filming, and he was also fully conscious during the entire procedure. He had the piece of skin tanned like leather (with the hairs still attached) and incorporated it into a 24-carat gold ring, the *Forget Me Knot*. The ring can be considered the ultimate example of Recht's working method and design vision. Recht is averse to mass production and prefers what he calls 'non-products', objects that can only be made in very small production runs, either by hand or with the help of simple machines. He also works exclusively with local materials. Recht does not avoid controversy,

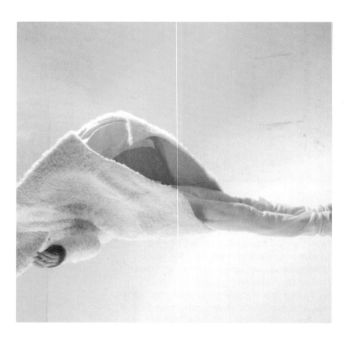

A

B

Exhibition
— *Carapace*
   Circumsolar collection,
   spring/summer 2013
   Translucent leather
   (vest made of facet-cut
   layers of lambskin)
   50 × 60 × 30 cm

A *When Gravity Fails*,
   autumn/winter 2011-2012.
   Photography: Marino Thorlacius
B-C *Carapace* from *the Circumsolar*
   collection, spring/summer 2013.
   Photography: Marino Thorlacius

and he is constantly searching for where the borders lie between fashion, art and performance.

The Israeli-born Recht grew up in Australia and has chosen Reykjavik as his base of operations. He works a great deal with the furs and skins of animals from the North Pole region, such as seals, arctic foxes, minke whales, dolphins, lambs, horses and fish. But he also likes to use concrete, wood, cardboard, wool and carbon – an essential element of all living things – not least because they are indigenous to the local area.

Iceland isn't just a convenient place to live for Recht. He feels a great affinity with the holistic culture of the Icelanders: they

throw away as little as possible and use almost every part of the animals they raise or hunt. His own methods of production are closely attuned to this approach. Recht makes extensive use of laser engravers and water jet cutters, for example, which are not only fast but are also extremely precise, so there's hardly any wastage. In most countries this would be far too costly, but in Iceland, with its clean geothermal energy, such a means of production is not out of the question. Because of these kinds of advanced cutting techniques Recht can spend much more time modelling. He often does this by hand, starting with a large piece of material that he drapes around a mannequin. For the collection *When Gravity Fails*,

he had the draping filmed by a camera. The images were then magnified and projected onto a wall, then transposed to paper, scanned, and finally cut by means of a laser. In Recht's work, traditional and highly advanced techniques and materials always go hand in hand and result in work – like the transparent *Carapace* vest – that is both futuristic and deeply rooted in local traditions.

c

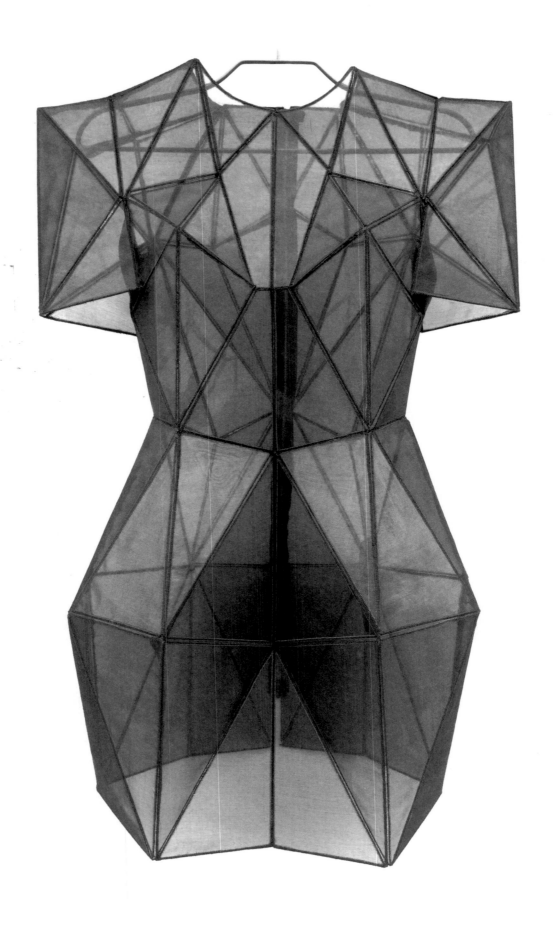

A

Irina Shaposhnikova's graduation collection *Crystallographica* grew out of her interest in the geological formation of crystals and minerals, which she used as the basis for creating new forms for the female body. She approached her work more as a sculptor than as a fashion designer, slowly building up an infrastructure of polygons, crystals and a finely knitted, high-tech fabric. Between the layers of fabric Shaposhnikova placed flexible plastic plates of varying thicknesses, enabling her to play with the light and material's transparency. The plates also make the designs highly wearable, resulting in a garment that moves gracefully with the body. *Crystallographica*, as we see in the dress that is being exhibited, is built up of a few hundred plastic triangular and polygonal forms. This labour-intensive approach cost Shaposhnikova many hours of work, also because she built a model for each design before starting to work with the actual material. The end result is a series of futuristic designs that reveal a completely new female image, but here and there they also recall the work of the Russian Futurists, an art movement from the early twentieth century that was inspired by the dynamism and restlessness of urban life with its rapid modernisation.

Material, texture and sculptural forms are also what guided Irina Shaposhnikova in her earlier work. For *Vivian Girls*, the graduation collection she created for her bachelor's degree from the Royal Academy of Fine Arts in Antwerp in 2009, Shaposhnikova made a series of knitted pieces in which she played with the conventions of the classic knitted sweater. She created cable sweaters with turtlenecks but replaced the material between the decorative cables – which is traditionally just plain wool – with a transparent beige or grey fabric, revealing the body beneath the sweater. She also increased the size of the cables, making it look as if the wearer of the woollen sweater was caught in a knitted cage. In addition to the cable sweaters Irina Shaposhnikova also made a few necklaces from woollen cables.

Irina Shaposhnikova

Irina Shaposhnikova (1984, Moscow, Russia) became interested in fashion at an early age. When she was fourteen she began spending time in her father's sewing studio, where she learned about materials and techniques. Shaposhnikova earned both a bachelor's and a master's degree from the Royal Academy of Fine Arts in Antwerp, from which she graduated in 2009. In 2011 the popular pop singer Lady Gaga appeared on the cover of the French magazine *Madame Figaro* in a design from the *Crystallographica* collection. At the moment Irina Shaposhnikova is working as an independent fashion designer.

1984 F ● Russia

Exhibition
— *Crystallographica*
  (1 garment)
  2009
  Transparent 100% silk
  organza, plastic
  120 × 100 × 100 cm

A   *Crystallographica*,
    top of the garment, 2009.
    Photography: Irina
    Shaposhnikova
B   *Crystallographica*, 2009.
    Model: Merel Wessing.
    Photography: Zed Daemen

Shao Yen
Shao Yen Chen

1981

M

● Taiwan

Shao Yen Chen (1981, Yilan, Taiwan) was converted to fashion after having been trained as a metal-worker and jewellery designer. In 2003 he began studying at the Central Saint Martins College of Art and Design in London, and did an internship with Alexander McQueen and Hussein Chalayan. His collection *Body as Clothes* was awarded the Fashion Weekend / Le Vif Award in Brussels in 2009. In 2010 Chen earned his master's degree and launched his own label under the name Shao Yen. Since 2010 his collections have been shown at every edition of the London Fashion Week. Shao Yen is regularly asked to help with special projects, such as decorating a shop window of Selfridges department store in London in February 2011.

www.shao-yen.com
www.vimeo.com/16119742
www.vimeo.com/22467845

Exhibition
— *Waver*
(2 dresses)
autumn/winter 2010-2011
Knitted cashmere, lycra, nylon
170 × 80 × 90 cm

A

A   *Waver* in *Centrefold Magazine* no. 6, 2010. Art director: Daniel Baer. Stylist: Joana Schlenzka. Models: Johanna Dray and Veronique Severe, Plus by Contrebande. Photography: Johan Sandberg
B   *Waver* at the MA graduation show of Central Saint Martins, 2010. Photography: Christopher Moore, Catwalking.com
C   *Waver* in the Mykromag-blog, 2011. Model: Raschelle Osbourne, Models1. Photography: Paul Scala

The Taiwanese designer Shao Yen Chen wasn't the least bit interested in fashion in his youth. He just wore the clothes his mother bought for him and studied metal-working and jewellery design. Yet at the end of the nineties he became intrigued by the sculptural designs of Issey Miyake and Yohji Yamamoto, and especially those of Rei Kawakubo (Comme des Garçons). Her collection *Body Becomes Dress Becomes Body* of 1997 made an enormous impression on Chen, which is reflected in his elegant, dazzling white collection *Waver* from 2010. Like Kawakubo, Chen dresses his models in garments that are covered in bulges, bulges that bear no relationship to the body whatsoever, and he does this deliberately to raise questions about the garment-body relationship. Large quantities of nylon threads create enormous volumes that change the natural forms of the arms, stomach and breasts into something unrecognisable. The body disappears entirely into the design. Chen himself says that the forms were inspired by the waves that crash on the shore of his birthplace, Yilan.

Another thing he likes to play with in his designs is the relationship between different materials. Chen effortlessly combines coarsely knitted fabrics with much

68

B

C

finer and more delicate materials like lycra and cashmere. Materials are always the point of departure in his work. He experiments with them endlessly and without any preconceived plans, just long enough for the design to gradually take shape. He always uses traditional techniques and skills that he learned as a metalworker, and he makes most of his creations himself, by hand.

The theatrical pieces by Shao Yen Chen look more as if they had been made for the stage or for photo shoots than for daily wear in the office or on the street. So it's not surprising that an eccentric artist like Björk has already asked him to make a dress

especially for her, or that Lady Gaga has shown an interest in working with him in the future. The dress being displayed at *The Future of Fashion is Now* was also made on commission. Director Alexandra McGuiness asked Chen to make a dress for her leading lady in the film *Lotus Eaters* (2011), which is about a group of hip Londoners wrestling with the problems of life and love.

Olek
Agata Oleksiak

1978

F

● Poland

Olek, whose real name is Agata Oleksiak (1978, Stachow, Poland) earned her bachelor's degree in Cultural Studies from Adam Mickiewicz University in Poznan, Poland, and then went to America to continue her studies at LaGuardia Community College in Queens, New York. There she won the National Arts Club Award for her crocheted sculptures. In 2005 Olek completed a residency in *Sculpture Space* in New York, in 2009 she did the same in the Instituto Sacatar in Brazil and in 2010 in AAI-LES in New York. In 2008 she won the Apex Art competition. In 2010 Olek was commissioned by the Brooklyn Museum of Art to create a one-day interactive performance installation. In 2012 Olek was part of the exhibition *40 Under 40: Craft Futures* in the Smithsonian Institution in Washington, where a completely crocheted apartment was on display.

www.oleknyc.com

A   *If men could get pregnant, abortion would be a sacrament*, International Women's Day, London, 2014
B   *Knitting is for Pus*****, 2010-2013.
Photography: Jeffrey Kilmer

Just one look beyond the cheerful colours and shapes of Olek's crocheting tells you that the yarns are meant to convey a whole range of socially critical messages. Olek uses her crocheted sculptures and installations to explore female sexuality, feminist ideals and the evolution of communication, and she also expresses her solidarity with the oppressed peoples of the world. She is constantly pushing the borders of fashion, art and craft. Because most of her work is presented out of doors in public spaces, the public also becomes involved. In this way Olek tries to bring about a gradual transformation in the way people think. Within this context she sees crocheting as a metaphor for the complexity and solidarity of our body and our spirit. The crocheted item is strong as a single unit, but as soon as a thread comes loose the entire work unravels.

Olek finds inspiration in other things besides these social themes. The enormous size of her crocheted pieces requires her to spend hours at a time crocheting, often with a film playing in the background. 'Life and art are inseparable. The movies I watch while crocheting influence my work, and my work dictates the films I select. I crochet everything that enters my space. Sometimes it's a text message, a medical report, found objects. There is the unravelling, the ephemeral part of my work that never lets me forget about the limited life of the art object and art concept.'[1]

Characteristic of Olek's almost maniacal way of working is her first solo exhibition *Knitting is for Pus*****, which was held at the Christopher Henry Gallery in New York. The exhibition shows Olek's fantasy world, in which hundreds of metres of crocheted and woven materials cover the gallery space from floor to ceiling. Visitors were invited to follow the yarns outside beginning in the gallery, and with the help of a map designed by Olek they could discover new crocheted sculptures on display throughout the neighbourhoods of NOLITA (NOrth of Little ITAly) and the Lower East Side.

A more modest approach – but not in terms of message – is the recent work *If men could get pregnant, abortion would be a sacrament*, which Olek created for International Women's Day 2014 for the Stolen Space Gallery in London. In a metres-long crocheted 'wall painting', Olek incorporated the slogan, 'If men could get pregnant, abortion would be a sacrament'.

1   See www.oleknyc.com/about

B

The Conversation

I proposed to create a life-sized, fully-crocheted skeleton that is an expression of my exploration of human identity and provides a commentary on the materiality of the human body and its interaction with fashion and design. My crocheted skeleton is a reflection on the form of the human body. Fashion and design often highlight the most flattering aspects of the human form while hiding those aspects or features seen by many as less desirable. By crocheting a complete, to-scale skeleton, I highlight the human body's most primal contours and elements.The skeleton turns the spotlight on what lies beneath the clothing while still shaping it. I uses high-quality acrylic yarn with metallic detailing to define the shape that informs the individual's identity.

The technique of crocheting chose me. When I was a little girl, there was nothing in the department store. My mother's brother, who lives in Rochester, NY, used to send us parcels [to Poland]. At that time, any goods found in the packages were confiscated. He started to send us fabric... lots of beautiful, colourful fabric.

It was impossible to purchase nice clothes, or any clothes at all. But it was very easy to find a seamstress. I had the most amazing wardrobe, but it was so different that I started to be treated as an outcast. But the point of the story is: my parents made me crochet little socks in exchange for the fabric. We would send them back to USA. My work was here long before I crossed the border.

Like... haha, not really.
Here is the real version. Clearly, my parents didn't make me crochet socks. That is just a joke ;-)

I started to crochet while writing my university thesis, *Symbolism of costumes in films by Peter Greenaway*. The thesis was the starting point for crocheting and film for me, but I actually only realized this insight a couple of years ago when I re-read it. Greenaway's references to Vermeer and Velazquez, the ideas of transforming old into new, and observing that everything was at some point previously made, continues to influence how I perceive art. I believe that we have to learn how to recreate and transform the world into art, and art into our world.

Loop after loop, hour after hour, my madness becomes crochet. Life and art are inseparable. The movies I watch while crocheting influence my work, and my work dictates the films I select. For this particular exhibition, I am choosing fashion movies, especially documentaries about fashion icons.

How does a thought or idea form itself? It is a response to information, images, words, food or lovers you have had... Inspiration comes from real life, as my camouflage pieces come to me from my own obsession with wearing different coloured camouflage pants. I wore camo pants the first time I came to the USA, and working with camo seemed like an extension of myself. I started crocheting, as I could not afford anything else. In 2002, I crocheted between trees because they were around me. I covered a stepladder because my ex-girlfriend had one and I was bored when she was working. Inspiration comes from life's innumerable details. Everything in my work comes from real feelings, experiences and intuition. These small details eventually build themselves up into greater statements. My installations are and have always been expressions of my responses to immediate surroundings, international climate, information, images, events in the news, emotions, words, lovers. These responses are what start the conversations that flow through my subconscious and through everyone else's. Ideas are collaborations between environment and time.

The public may not know the background story; they accept it or even love my work because it is honest. I hope.

I believe in developing new ways of creating a dialogue with the viewer on both visual and aural levels. All of the five senses are heightened as the audience develops new means of interacting with the piece, realising that their response greatly impacts the art and the ways these forms are moving over time. Their response is the art, and my work is a mirror.

My art explores sexuality, feminist ideals, pressing environmental issues and the evolution of communication through colours, conceptual exploration and meticulous detail. I consistently push the boundaries between fashion, art, craft and public art, fluidly combining the sculptural and the fanciful. With the old fashion technique of crocheting, I have taken the ephemeral medium of yarn to express everyday occurrences, inspirations and hopes to create a metaphor for the complexity and interconnectedness of our physical and psychological processes.

Olek

A-B-C
The Conversation,
process images, 2014.
Photography: Olek
D *The Conversation*, 2014.
Photography: Kristy Leibowitz

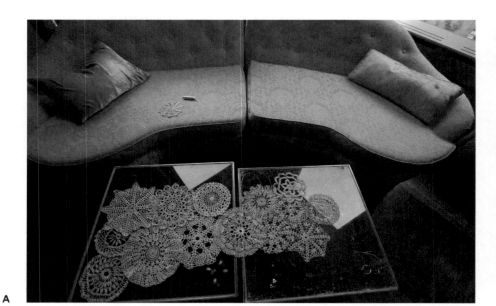

A

c

Iris van Herpen

F   1984

● The Netherlands

Iris van Herpen (1984, Wamel, the Netherlands) is seen as one of the most innovative designers of her generation. She earned her bachelor's degree in fashion design from the ArtEZ Institute of the Arts in Arnhem in 2006. In 2007 she started her own label. In July 2011 Van Herpen was admitted to the prestigious Chambre Syndicale de la Haute Couture. During the same year, Iris van Herpen was also the focus of the exhibition *Het Nieuwe Ambacht* in the Centraal Museum in Utrecht, where her designs were shown side by side with her sources of inspiration. The Groninger Museum held a retrospective of her work in 2012.

www.irisvanherpen.com

Ever since Iris van Herpen started her own fashion label in 2007 things have been moving fast for her. Her unique way of working – a combination of labour-intensive handiwork and new technologies like 3D printing – produces impressive designs that are all the result of Van Herpen's research on the female body and how fashion relates to that body. One decisive factor in the design process is movement: even though Iris van Herpen works with rigid materials like plastic, metal and wood, her designs must move along with the body in a fluid line. '"Form follows function" is not a slogan with which I concur', says Van Herpen. 'On the contrary, I find that forms complement and change the body and thus the emotion.'[1]

One of the high points in the oeuvre of the young designer is the *Escapism* couture collection, which was presented in Paris in January 2011. For this collection Van Herpen worked with the English architect Daniel Widrig, and MGX BY MATERIALISE took care of the practical execution of the designs by means of 3D printing and selective laser sintering.[2] The theme of the collection is the fact that many people are losing sight of reality because of the presence of so many digital media, and that the very same digital media often

B

C

create an insatiable hunger for more. Van Herpen was also inspired by the exuberant sculptures of the American artist Kris Kuksi. All this resulted in a collection of dramatic pieces in which the fragile, 3D-printed designs contrasted sharply against the dark, spherical dresses that were constructed of hundreds of loose strips.

Van Herpen's regular womenswear collections also make an impression. *Embossed Sounds* (spring/summer 2014) contains garments that make noise when they're touched. And for the collection *Biopiracy* (autumn/winter 2014-2015), Iris van Herpen worked with artist Malstaf to create an unusual catwalk presentation. Several models were almost completely shrink-wrapped in large plastic bags and hung in a foetal position, while other models paraded down the catwalk. As the show progressed, the shrink-wrapped models changed position. For this collection, Iris van Herpen found inspiration in the fact that it's possible today to take out a patent on genes. This caused her to wonder whether our bodies are still our property, and what individual freedom really means.

1   See www.irisvanherpen.com/about
2   In this process, the printer creates the outside of the design and fills in the hollow interior with powder. This powder is hardened into a massive product by means of a laser, layer after layer. Finally the form is sandblasted for a neat finish.

A-B-C
Biopiracy, mixture of *ready-to-wear* and couture collection, autumn/winter 2014-2015. Photography: Michel Zoeter

Ferro Fluid Dress

With a combination of delicate handwork, digital technologies and innovative materials, Van Herpen creates refined collections that often have a futuristic touch. She uses 3D-printed, interactive clothing to explore the ways that new technologies can impact form and movement. In *Ferro Fluid Dress* the designer places a doll wearing a 3D-printed dress in a bath of black fluid.

'The 3D-printed dress has a structure of open lines in the waist on which ferriferous fluid is dripped from above. Magnets cause the fluid to stay on the waist of the dress rather than drip into the bathwater. Because the dress is constantly and subtly being turned, it seems to grow whenever the drops fall on it.'

Iris van Herpen

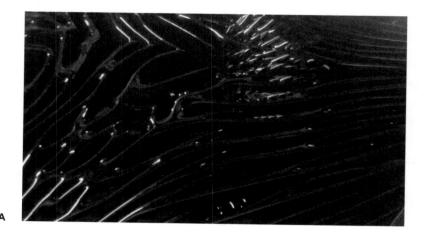

A

B

A-B Video stills of the design
process of *Ferro Fluid Dress*,
installation, 2014.
Video: Iris van Herpen and
Jolan van der Wiel
C *Ferro Fluid Dress*,
sketch, 2014

The (Re)Definition of the Human Figure

José Teunissen

The fashion system has a multitude of trends and clothing styles to choose from, but the underlying beauty ideal – young and size 32 – is extremely coercive and rigid. Many young designers see it as a challenge to break free of these shackles. That is happening in a number of ways. On the one hand there are designers like Movana Chen (China) and Minna Palmqvist (Finland), who call the system into question and show how coercive and manipulative the ideals of beauty are and how distant they are from reality. On the other hand, designers like Craig Green (United Kingdom) and Si Chan (China) use humour and a playful imagination to stretch the borders of the ideal of classic beauty and to give us new ways of representing the human figure.

Craig Green,
spring/summer 2015

Craig Green, for example, designs outfits whose abstract sculptural and architectural qualities make them look more like comic strip figures, a house or a work of art. In doing so he opens up new possibilities for the human form that stimulate subconscious fantasies and longings, going beyond the expression of individual or group identity that we normally demonstrate with our clothing. In Green's work, the influence of designer Walter Van Beirendonck (with whom he had an internship) is clearly recognisable. Francesca Granata connected the work of Walter Van Beirendonck with the grotesque body as alluded to by the Renaissance writer and humanist Rabelais: 'The grotesque body is a body in the act of becoming. It is never finished, never completed; it is continually being built, created, and in turn continually builds and creates another body.'[1] For years, Van Beirendonck has shown how the human figure can be linked to fantasies and experiences that are very different from those we usually see, fantasies that in the culture of the eighteenth century in particular, with its balls, carnival and masquerades, were considered quite normal.[2]

Designers like Craig Green, but also Si Chan, who gave literal expression to the human embrace with his *Hug Me* collection, are not satisfied with simply making the body fashionable, giving it an identity and a personality; they also want to investigate the experiences, fantasies and meanings that the clothed human figure can convey, as well as the effect that can be produced by the external form. In doing so they place themselves – as far as fashion is concerned – in the tradition of *Lumps and Bumps* from 1997 by Rei Kawakubo (Japan), who far exceeded the limits of what was considered good fashion taste at the time by giving her clothing curves in unusual places. In doing so she showed that unexpected volumes may create an interesting sculptural effect but they're also seen as repellent by the fashion world because they're associated with 'deformity'. Apparently small variations in body shapes awaken our anxieties and bizarre fantasies at a very primitive level, and this aspect is only reinforced when placed within the straitjacket of fashion ideals. 'In its lack of fixity, stability and order the grotesque – excessive and uncontainable – clashes with the canon of the beautiful upheld by traditional art history and classical aesthetics, which is characterised by proportionality, symmetry and order', Granata says.[3]

This is exactly the question that motivates young avant-garde fashion designers: can we take fashion beyond its strict ideals of beauty, and do it in a playful way by simply experimenting with body shapes? For what lies hidden behind a person or identity in a globalised, secularised society in which we see ourselves as both world citizens and as part of the local community, and in which we have both a real life and a digital existence on the internet? In this fundamentally altered society, it's no accident that today's designers are trying to rediscover the visual 'identity' and function of fashion by looking into the meaning and effect of the body. Forrest Jessee (United States) provides a fine example of this with his *Sleep Suit* project (2010), which developed out of a design assignment to create a sleeping place in a large public area. 'Every project starts by dropping all assumptions and undergoes a process of rethinking,' Jessee says. With *Sleep Suit* one can sleep anywhere, even in public spaces, because the material is reinforced in essential places. By turning sleeping into a public ritual instead of an activity for private spaces, Jessee creates a garment with new values and applications that is both logical and functional.

Designers and artists such as Pyuupiru (Japan), Imme van der Haak (the Netherlands) and Minna Palmqvist (Finland) work with the same experimental attitude regarding the representation of the body; they are particularly interested in revealing the

Pyuupiru, *Earth* from the *Planetaria* series, 2000

limitations of the rigid ideals of beauty. Pyuupiru's performances focus on her transformation from a man to a woman, thereby demonstrating that a human body can be visually moulded into either a feminine or a masculine identity. Imme van der Haak illustrates how clothing, body and identity can blend seamlessly together in the video installation *Beyond the Body: A Perception of Appearance and Identity* from 2012. In this work, images of bodies and faces on transparent clothing gradually converge or change into the bodies and faces of the wearers as they move. Where does one person end and the other begin?

Birgit Dieker (Germany) demonstrates the power and significance of clothing in a rather grim way by transforming unwashed second-hand clothing into human sculptures. Openings and indentations literally reveal the layers of clothing and with them the human figure's layers of identity.

Imme van der Haak,
*Beyond the Body:
A Perception of
Appearance and
Identity*, 2012

Movana Chen (China) sees clothing as a form of self-expression and as the most accessible way to create identity, but she criticises the rules that fashion imposes by tearing fashion magazines into strips, which she uses to knit *body containers* that she calls 'magazine clothes'. 'My attempt is to explore various methods to "wear" one's identity,' says Chen in addressing the relationship between clothing and the fashion media.[4] Minna Palmqvist (Finland) levels the same criticism at the fashion straitjacket with her installation *Intimately Social* (2009). She blows up the contours of the human figure with balloons to create different silhouettes. In this way she underscores the friction between the ideal body pre-

Birgit Dieker, *Ei, Ei, Ei*
(self-portrait), 2010

sented in the fashion world and the bodies that most women actually possess. These designers show – always in a unique way – how the relationship develops between body, clothing, fashion and identity and how restrictive today's fashion system is in that regard. When it comes to the connection between body, aesthetics and identity, fashion today is reinventing itself.

1   Michail Bakhtin, *Rabelais and his World*, Bloomington, IN 1984, p. 317.
2   Philippe Perrot, *Le travail des apparences: Ou les transformations du corps féminin XVIIIe-XIXe siècle*, Paris, 1984.
3   Francesca Granata, 'Fashion of Inversion: The Carnivalesque and the Grotesque in Contemporary Belgian Fashion', in: Nele Bernheim (ed.), *Symposium 1: Modus Operandi: State of Affairs in Current Research on Belgian Fashion*, ModeMuseum, Antwerp 2008, pp. 17-35, q.v. p. 37.
4   See www.movanachen.com/pf_as.htm

Comme des Garçons
Rei Kawakubo

1942

F

■ Japan

The Japanese fashion label Comme des Garçons was founded by Rei Kawakubo (1942, Tokyo, Japan) in 1973. Kawakubo studied art and literature at the University of Keio. She then worked a few years for a textile company. With her label Comme des Garçons, Rei Kawakubo was one of the first to present radically new fashion in the eighties. Today Comme des Garçons has grown into a fashion empire that brings out a perfume line in addition to women's, men's and children's fashion. Kawakubo and her husband Adrian Joffe are also the founders of Dover Street Market, a series of warehouses in Tokyo, London and New York. Dover Street Market sells its own products as well as other innovative fashion and design.

www.comme-des-garcons.com

Exhibition
— *Lumps and Bumps*
spring/summer 1997
Two-piece suit: nylon, polyurethane, down
Skirt: 70 × 35 cm, waist: 30 cm
Blouse: 85 × 35 cm
Collection of Museum Boijmans Van Beuningen, Rotterdam

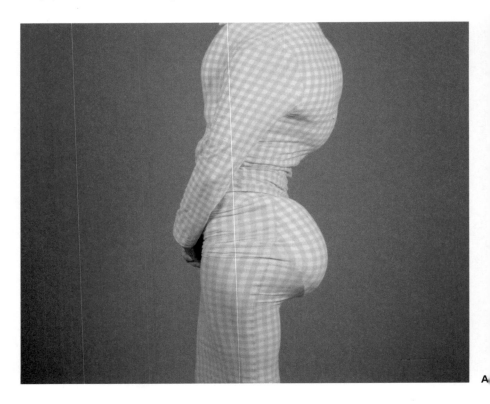

A

A   *Lumps and Bumps*, two-piece suit, spring/summer 1997. Photography: Museum Boijmans Van Beuningen
B   *Lumps and Bumps*, jacket, spring/summer 1997. Photography: Gerrit Schreurs, The Hague

Although Rei Kawakubo is seen as one of today's most groundbreaking fashion designers, her innovative, unusual creations did not always go down well. She undermines all the Western ideals of beauty and femininity. The fashion press described her first collection, which Kawakubo presented on the Paris catwalk in 1981, as a 'post-Hiroshima look' because the predominance of black made it look so depressing. Rei Kawakubo's designs express her criticism of the way the established fashion world depicts feminine beauty. She emphasises that she designs for independent women who are able to attract men with their minds and not with their bodies.[1] She is also eager to denounce the concept of 'fashion'. By making use of unfinished hems, by exposing the construction of a garment and playing with forms, Rei Kawakubo tries to give the fashion public something to think about.

One of the most widely discussed collections that Rei Kawakubo produced for Comme des Garçons is the *Lumps and Bumps* collection from the summer of 1997. This collection consists of dresses made of translucent chiffon and pastel checked motifs that are padded with cushions on the buttocks, shoulders and back, giving them an entirely new shape. *Body Becomes Dress Becomes Body* was the statement that Kawakubo released with this collection, which was an attack on symmetry in Western fashion. By placing the cushion-like bumps at random places on the female body, Kawakubo was encouraging people to ask themselves whether symmetry was

a necessary ingredient of beauty. A British fashion journalist wrote this about the collection: 'The first model walked out with a sheer black stretch top, a hump over her bottom and knitted pads shoved down the back of her top, to make her look like a cross between Elephant Man, Quasimodo and the eccentric night-clubber, performance artist and Lucian Freud model Leigh Bowery.'[2] Another journalist wrote about the collection: 'Does she mean tumours?'[3]

Today the *Lumps and Bumps* collection from Comme des Garçons is regarded as a milestone in fashion history. For the first time, a female body was presented on the catwalk that departed radically from the anatomical form; breasts were hidden from view by the placement of big bumps on the back, and hips disappeared under mounds of cushions.

1   Amy de la Haye, '"*A Dress is No Longer a Little Flat Closed Thing*": Issey Miyake, Rei Kawakubo, Yohji Yamamoto & Junya Watanabe', in: Claire Wilcox (ed.), *Radical Fashion*, London 2001, p. 31.
2   See www.guardian.co.uk/theobserver/2001/oct/07/features.magazine37
3   Caroline Evans, *Fashion at the Edge. Spectacle, Modernity and Deathliness*, New Haven/London, 2003, p. 269.

Hussein Chalayan's roots lie in the divided Cyprus, where Greek Christians and Turkish Muslims live on opposite sides of the border and, in the mainly Islamic environment he grew up in, another border runs between men and women. This theme can be seen in almost all of Chalayan's designs. He presented his autumn/winter 2000-2001 collection *After Words* in a living room, for example, where the coffee table could be transformed into a skirt and the furniture upholstery into dresses. 'What do you do when you suddenly have to flee – for political or religious reasons or for any reason at all

– and you have no time to pack your things?' was the question Hussein Chalayan was asking with his design. The question is still relevant today, and it's a situation he himself has experienced.

Hussein Chalayan's collection for spring/summer 2008, entitled *Readings*, is also quite impressive. Chalayan worked with Swarovski on a few of the dresses in the collection. *Readings* was not presented in a traditional catwalk show but in a short film by Nick Knight and Ruth Hogben on the SHOWstudio website. The film shows the models standing on a revolving platform

Hussein Chalayan

Hussein Chalayan (1970, Nicosia, Cyprus) was born in Turkish Cyprus but moved with his family to England in 1978. There Chalayan graduated from the Central Saint Martins College of Art and Design in London in 1993 with the collection _The Tangent Flows_, which contained garments that he had dusted with metal and buried in his garden, then dug up to see how they had been affected. Chalayan was unlike any of his fellow students at Saint Martins: ideas interested him more than clothing. In 1994 he launched his own label. Many different disciplines are combined in his designs such as anthropology, technology and philosophy, which has quickly earned him the label 'fashion intellectual'. Hussein Chalayan has participated in many exhibitions with his work.

www.chalayan.com

<u>Exhibition</u>
— _Laser Dress_
  Readings collection,
  spring/summer 2008
  Dress made of cotton,
  organza, Swarovski crystals
  and integrated laser diodes
  Sisal hat with integrated
  laser diodes
  c. 270 × 215 × 125 cm
  Collection of Museum Boijmans
  Van Beuningen, Rotterdam,
  loaned by Han Nefkens Fashion
  on the Edge, 2010

B

A   C

with laser beams shining on their faces. Chalayan used the Swarovski crystals to reflect the beams. He incorporated about a hundred crystals into each design. The crystals are mounted on hinges which allow them to move. As a result they're not just static objects but they keep changing form, interacting with the space in which they're placed.

Hussein Chalayan found inspiration for this collection in the sun gods and sun worshippers of the ancient religions as well as in today's celebrity culture. The laser beams represent the relationship between public

and icon. Visitors to the website could select their own music for the film from a pre-selection put together by singer Antony Hegarty from Antony and the Johnsons.

This is the second time that Hussein Chalayan has participated in an exhibition initiated by Han Nefkens Fashion on the Edge in Museum Boijmans Van Beuningen. In 2009 Chalayan created the work _Micro Geography: A Cross Section_ for the exhibition _The Art of Fashion_.

A-B-C
   Laser Dress from the _Readings_
   collection, spring/summer 2008.
   Video: Nick Knight/SHOWstudio.
   Photography: Nick Knight

Si Chan

Si Chan (1989, Macau, China) grew up in Macau, near Hong Kong, and moved to London after secondary school in order to study fashion design at the London College of Fashion. Chan graduated in the summer of 2012, specialising in menswear with the collection *Hug Me*. This colourful collection received a great deal of press attention. At the moment Si Chan is working on his master's degree in menswear at Central Saint Martins in London.

Exhibition
— *Hug Me* collection
   (2 garments)
   2012
   Fabric (nylon, lining material, mixed materials)
   56 × 90 cm and 60 × 120 cm

The graduation collection *Hug Me* by Si Chan is all about the disconnect between people and the loneliness that it produces. This is a personal theme for Si Chan, who felt very isolated during his years of study at the London College of Fashion because of the fierce competition among the students there. He was also homesick for his family and friends in Hong Kong. With the words 'Everybody needs love, don't you?' in the back of his head, Si Chan designed six outfits, each one with its own story to tell. One distinctive feature of the collection is the hands that are worked into every design, culminating in the series of hands and arms that are converted into a cape. In creating this collection, Si Chan wanted to show how important it is to hug someone every now and then: 'Interaction and communication are actions to express love and depart from human beings' loneliness. People's lives in

A

B

cities are gradually losing something that should be treasured primitively. A hug is just a simple action but represents the importance of living together.'[1] To emphasise what it feels like to be hugged, the hands and arms are stuffed and incorporated into the clothing, where they hold the wearer in a strong embrace around the waist, shoulders and neck. There are even fingers in the shoes.

Although Si Chan's designs are avant-garde and very personal in nature, they are also exceptionally wearable – a basic requirement, according to the designer. Today's fashion system is too impersonal, says Chan. He hopes to bring about changes in this regard with his designs, and to explore the borders between fashion and art. The lookbook that Si Chan made for *Hug Me* with photographer Sara Pista is also quite

special. In her photography, Pista wanted to underscore the loneliness experienced by the residents of the big city. To do this she shot the clothing at several different abandoned spots in London, using invisible models. The result does justice to Chan's surrealistic designs and conveys his message – hug me! – in a convincing and moving way.

1   See www.monsieurjerome.com/now-sileongchan/#1

A-B-C
Hug Me collection, 2012.
Photography: Sara Pista

The purpose of Movana Chen's *Body Container* (2010) is to examine the relationship between clothing and the media while reflecting on our consumption of throwaway goods. For *Body Container*, Chen shredded stacks of paper into tiny strips and knitted them together to form a 'container' that literally covers the body from head to toe. At first she used only fashion magazines, but later she also added newspapers, maps, books and her own diaries. She chose fashion magazines because many people see fashion as the most accessible way to express one's identity. But at the same time Chen believes that fashion is also the perfect means for restricting personal expression: fashion determines which styles are acceptable – 'fashionable' – and which ones are not. Aesthetics are rarely taken into account. Fashion magazines play a key role here: they tell us what to wear if we want to appear fashionable. What Movana Chen wants to do with her work is to break through the power of these fashion magazines and to show us that underneath the layers of clothing featured in them there are real people.

'Through the knitting of these multi-languages hidden with the magazine papers, we learn about communication. My attempt is to explore the various methods to "wear" one's identity, to experiment and play with

it, to create new opportunities for different cultures and identities and to begin the communication between one another. The reconstructed paper pieces represent wishes, and are transformed into meanings about daily life,' according to Movana Chen.[1] The public doesn't even need to understand the words that are printed on the strips of paper; the mere act of looking at the *Body Container* implies communication. In this way, Chen says, the borders of verbal communication are broken down and art is used as an accessible way of demonstrating that her work is connected to our daily lives. To make sure this expresses itself as a dialogue and not simply as one-way traffic, Movana Chen actually puts her *Body Container* on and takes it to the street. For some projects, Movana Chen tears up the books and magazines right on the spot, knitting the resulting strips of papers into a *Body Container*. In 2010 in Seoul, for example, Chen made a *Body Container* from torn books about Korean art and history, and in London in 2012 she created *Travel Maps*, a *Body Container* knitted from maps of London.

1   See www.movanachen.com/pf_as.htm

Movana Chen

Movana Chen (1974, Guandong, China) earned her Bachelor of Fine Arts degree from the Royal Melbourne Institute of Technology University in Hong Kong. She also studied at the London College of Fashion. In 2004 she began her knitting projects, using strips of paper to deconstruct and reconstruct the significance of printed matter. Movana Chen prefers a multidisciplinary approach that combines fashion, installation art, sculpture, media and performance. Her work has been shown at exhibitions in Hong Kong, London, Seoul, Beijing, Shanghai, Sicily, Philadelphia and Singapore. In 2007 Movana Chen represented Hong Kong at the Seoul Fringe Festival. In 2013 she had a solo exhibition, *KNITerature*, at Artis-Tree in Hong Kong.

www.movanachen.com

1974

V

● China

Exhibition
— ***Body Container – Travel Maps***
   2014
   Knitted, shredded roadmaps, e.g *ANWB Road Map the Netherlands*
   160 × 60 cm
— ***Body Container Comes to Life in Hong Kong***
   2013
   HD video: 18 minutes

A   *Body Container Comes to Life in Hong Kong*, 2013.
    Model: Movana Chen.
    Film: James Vyner
B   *Body Container Comes to Life in London*, 2012.
    Model: Movana Chen.
    Film: James Vyner
C   Movana Chen knitting in her studio, Hong Kong, 2013.
    Photography: Movana Chen

During the 1960s, sculptors began working with materials that were quite unusual for the time such as latex, felt, fabrics and even hair. These materials, which were regarded as cheap and ephemeral, were felt to be pre-eminently suitable for telling stories about the human body. The sculptures of Birgit Dieker are part of this tradition. She uses her work to question the prevailing ideals of beauty and the social roles we play in society. Dieker is not interested in superficial beauty. Her aim is to expose what's going on inside. Her sculptures are an effort to examine both perfection and destruction.

To this end Birgit Dieker works mostly with used clothing. Most of it is donated, and sometimes she buys materials in second-hand shops or at flea markets. First she unpicks the seams from the garment, then she drapes the pieces around a wooden form. She does this over and over again, as she did in *Arme* (2011), and then sews every layer onto the previous layer to keep the sculpture from falling apart when she begins to cut. This cutting exposes the various layers from which the sculpture is constructed and makes them visible to the public. In this way the aesthetically perfect surface reveals its emotional wounds. According to Dieker, the use of familiar materials in this debate between the perfect surface and the mutilated interior sets off a playful dialogue among members of the public that relates directly to their own physiques.

Dieker's decision to work mostly with clothing makes perfect sense to her. The clothes we wear become a second skin, and because we decide for ourselves what

we're going to put on, our clothing says something about who we are. By using garments for her sculptures, Birgit Dieker is trying to say something about the many layers of our identity. This is also one of the reasons why she only works with second-hand, unwashed clothes. She believes that in this way the history of the wearer remains attached to the material.

Birgit Dieker

Birgit Dieker (1969, Gescher, Germany) studied German language and literature at the Technical University of Berlin, then enrolled in a programme in art education at the Institute of the Arts. She went on to earn a master's degree in sculpture before finally graduating in 1999. The focus of her work is the human body, which she repeatedly tries to alienate from the public by chopping it into bits and also by showing off the interior of the sculptures – the material that she uses to build up the sculptures.

www.birgit-dieker.de

<u>Exhibition</u>
— *Arme* (*Arms*)
2011
Second-hand garments
15 × 39 × 29 cm

1969

F

● Germany

B

A

A   *Arme*, 2011.
Photography: Jürgen Baumann
B   *Rosie*, 2007.
Photography: Marcus Schneider

Phyllis Galembo

1952

F

■ United States

Phyllis Galembo (1952, New York, United States) earned her Master of Fine Arts from the University of Wisconsin, Madison, and is a professor of art at the University at Albany, State University of New York. Her work has been exhibited many times, including at the International Center for Photography and the American Museum of Natural History in New York, the George Eastman House International Museum of Photography and Video in Rochester, NY, the Smithsonian National Museum of Natural History in Washington, DC, and in the exhibition *Masquerade, A Decade* at Galerie Alex Daniëls – Reflex in Amsterdam. Her photos have been purchased by museums such as the Metropolitan Museum of Art in New York, the Museum of Fine Arts in Houston, Albany Institute of History and Art, Philadelphia Museum of Art and the Schomberg Center for Research in Black Culture in New York. She has also published several books about her work. In 2014 Phyllis Galembo received a John Simon Guggenheim Fellowship for her work.

www.galembo.com

Exhibition
— *Akata Masquerade, Eshinjok Village, Nigeria*, 2004
  Carver: Adi Montung
— *Ekpo Masquerade, Calabar South, Nigeria*, 2005
  Costume maker: Edet Ekpo
— *Agbo Meji (Two rams never drink at the same time from one pot), Egungun Masquerade, Bohicon, Benin*, 2006
  Three colour photographs
  98 × 98 cm
  Galerie Alex Daniëls – Reflex Amsterdam

A *Agbo Meji (Two rams never drink at the same time from one pot), Egungun Masquerade, Bohicon, Benin*, 2006
B *Akata Masquerade, Eshinjok Village, Nigeria*, 2004
C *Ekpo Masquerade, Calabar South, Nigeria*, 2005

A

Phyllis Galembo photographs cultural and religious traditions in South America and Africa in countries such as Brazil, Jamaica, Cuba, Haiti, Benin and Nigeria. It was in this last country that she took the photo *10 Affianwan, Calabar South, Nigeria* (2005). In Galembo's work the emphasis is on the transformative power of religious clothing, particularly the clothing of masquerades worn in ritual performances. These performances are often connected to themes such as fertility, war, peace, illness and politics, which are also reflected in Galembo's portraits. Other themes represented in her work are dualities such as man and god,

power and oppression, and past and future.

Phyllis Galembo sees masquerade as a form of wearable art in which meaning is woven into the often extravagant clothing, transforming the wearer from an ordinary mortal to a divine being. This makes the ritual an expression of the cultural heritage of the wearer of the ritual clothing and masks as well as a divine experience: participants in these rituals believe that the spirits of the ancestors take possession of the body of the wearer. So it also frequently happens that Phyllis Galembo is required to ask permission of these spirits in order to photograph the ritual clothing, which she

B

does ceremonially. Although her photos appear staged, they're not at all. After Galembo receives permission to take the pictures she builds a small improvised set in which the lighting is particularly important, since good lighting guarantees that the often bright colours of the costumes will be properly recorded.

Phyllis Galembo's interest in ritual traditions began in 1985 when she visited Nigeria and the Ivory Coast for the first time to teach there for one summer. From that moment on, Galembo travelled there frequently and made many portraits of religious events and ceremonies. Galembo's

fascination with colourful costumes didn't come out of the blue: she's been intrigued by dressing up since she was a child. This explains why her favourite holiday is Halloween, and why Galembo herself has a collection of Halloween costumes that now numbers about five hundred.

Imme van der Haak

1987

F

● The Netherlands

Imme van der Haak (1987, Arnhem, the Netherlands) completed her training as a product designer at the ArtEZ Institute of the Arts in Arnhem in 2010. She followed this up with a master's degree in product design from the Royal College of Art in London, which she finished in 2012. In her work Imme van der Haak concentrates on the question 'what is normal?', in which she focuses on everyday life and all the things we put up with, doing it in a subtle, playful way. At the moment Imme van der Haak is working as an independent designer. In June 2013 her work *Beyond the Body: A Perception of Appearance and Identity* (2012) was shown at the *I Like To Watch Too* performance festival held at Paradiso in Amsterdam.

www.immevanderhaak.nl

Exhibition
— *Beyond the Body: A Perception of Appearance and Identity*
2012
Costumes (digitally printed silk) and performance video
c. 200 × 100 cm
Video: 2 minutes, 52 seconds

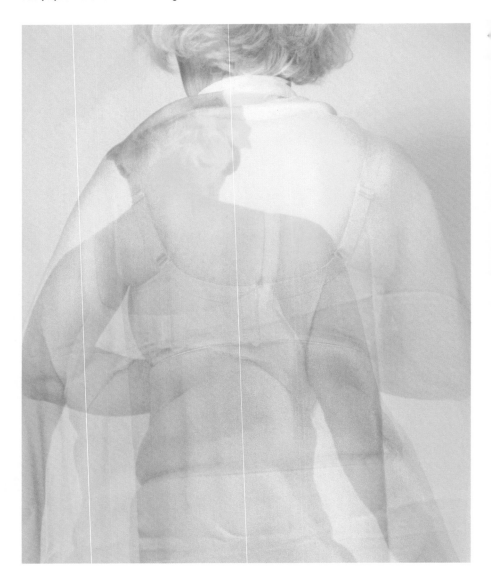

A-B *Beyond the Body: A Perception of Appearance and Identity*, 2012. Dancers: Alice Gaspari and Catherine Bell. Choreography: in cooperation with Alexandra Green. Film: Maja Zamodja

In her work *Beyond the Body: A Perception of Appearance and Identity* (2012) Imme van der Haak explores the physical forms of the human body and the question of physical limits: where does one person end and the other begin. The work is also a subtle criticism of the heavy retouching being done in fashion photography today. Van der Haak does all this by means of a simple intervention. *Beyond the Body* is a video featuring two dancers dressed in transparent silk garments. Printed on these garments – one is being exhibited next to the video – are life-sized photos of men and women of various ages. As the two dance, we see their bodies and faces slowly morph into the bodies and faces printed on the clothing. Where does one person end and the other begin? It's difficult to say; in the work of Imme van de Haak, body, age, generations and identity are all intertwined.

To emphasise this fact, Van der Haak created a flipbook to accompany the instal-

lation. Printed in the book are page after page of different faces, from young to old. When you flip through the book quickly the faces flow seamlessly together, and here, too, it's difficult to say where the one person ends and the other begins. As Imme van der Haak herself says about *Beyond the Body*: 'In a dance performance, the moving body manipulates the fabric so the body and the silk become one, distorting our perception or revealing a completely new physical form. The movement then brings this to life. *Beyond the Body* brings into being an ambiguous image that intrigues, astonishes or sometimes even disturbs.'

1   See www.immevanderhaak.nl/index.php?/ product/beyond-the-body/

A

In 2010 Forrest Jossee presented his *Sleep Suit* to the public. His inspiration for this design came from Buckminster Fuller's theory of 'Dymaxion Sleeping', which advocates adopting a sleep pattern of four short, thirty-minute sessions every six hours instead of one whole night of sleep. With his *Sleep Suit*, Jessee's aim was not only to redefine the sleep ritual but also to examine the roles of public and private space. As he himself describes it: 'Every project starts by dropping all assumptions and undergoes a process of rethinking.'

Forrest Jessee's *Sleep Suit* has its origin in a design assignment in which he was asked to create a sleeping area in a large, open space. While other architects immediately began by using conventional architectural language and designing walls, doors and windows to incorporate into their project, Forrest Jessee thought beyond a space's physical limits. In his design he combines architectural concepts such as demarcation, personal space and transparency with the requirements for a good night's sleep such as comfort, fresh air and sleep ritual. This resulted in a testing of materials that straddle the border between fashion and architecture. The *Sleep Suit* grew out of the architect's knowledge of structures combined with the three-dimensional pleating technique from the fashion world, resulting in a suit that is strong enough to bear the weight of a human body. Forrest Jessee sees the suit as a hybrid: half physical space and half fashion creation. It's an architectural structure that can be placed around the body, while at the same time (because it has to do with fashion) keeping the wearer's identity visible.

The *Sleep Suit* makes it possible for the wearer to sleep everywhere and anywhere – on the floor, in a chair behind the desk, in the train, on a bench in the park. The suit is made in such a way that it can absorb shocks; it's like a cocoon built around the body. Jessee's experimentation led him to discover where the body needs extra support, and he adapted the thickness of the foam layer in those places. The *Sleep Suit* has now undergone such extensive development that it can be produced in large quantities while remaining cost-effective.

Forrest Jessee

Forrest Jessee (1977, Richmond, VA, United States) studied at the Graduate School of Architecture, Planning and Preservation at Columbia University in New York. Upon graduating he was awarded a prize for his efforts as a student. A William Kinne Traveling Fellowship enabled him to do research in the rain forests of Brazil. He works on the cutting edge of fashion, graphic design, architecture and installation art. He has received commissions from the Graduate School of Design at Harvard University, Columbia University, Platforma Bogotá, Lille3000 and Diller Scofidio + Renfro. He works as an assistant adjunct professor at the Graduate School of Architecture, Planning and Preservation of Columbia University.

www.forrestjessee.com

1977

M

● United States

Exhibition
— *Sleep Suit*
   2010
   Laser-cut EVA foam
   200 × 100 × 100 cm

B

A *Sleep Suit* in the grass, 2010.
   Photography: © Forrest Jessee
B *Sleep Suit* series, 2010.
   Photography: © Forrest Jessee

A

The Finnish fashion designer Minna Palmqvist began *Intimately Social* in 2007 as a graduation project for her master's degree in Stockholm. It can be regarded as a running collection, with new designs being added several times a year. *Intimately Social* is far more than clothing; it also involves installation art and films. Palmqvist – who regards herself as a feminist – sees *Intimately Social* as a total art work in which the various parts support each other and reinforce her story.

According to Minna Palmqvist, *Intimately Social*, as the title suggests, is all about contrasts, especially the contrast between social identity and the individuality of women. The starting point for all her designs is the friction between the socially accepted female body and the constantly changing body of flesh and blood. As

Palmqvist explains, 'My garments get their inspiration from the exploitation of the female body within fashion and western society, and symbolize the meeting between the socially accepted body and the fleshy, ever changing body we actually have. It is a battle between what we wish for, and what we are trying to hide. The garments emerge from intimate garment details and unwanted body shapes, which enters the fashion scene without pardon.' Minna Palmqvist is also especially interested in the rules of today's fashion system, and she wonders how they can be changed to create a more sustainable future.

Featured in the exhibition *The Future of Fashion is Now* is the installation *Intimately Social 4.09* from 2009, taken from the *Intimately Social* collection. The installation

Minna Palmqvist

After graduating with a master's degree in textile from the Konstfack College of Arts, Crafts and Design in Stockholm in 2007, Minna Palmqvist (1980, Åland Islands, Finland) started her own label. There she elaborates on her graduation project *Intimately Social* and ignores the traditional fashion seasons. With *Intimately Social* she investigates our obsession with the female body by applying socially critical commentary to the fashions she makes. In 2011 Minna Palmqvist was nominated for the Swedish Mercedes Benz Young Fashion Industry Awards.

www.minnapalmqvist.com

<u>Exhibition</u>
— *Intimately Social 4.09*, from the series *Intimately Social* 2009
  Installation: balloons, leather and jersey knit garments, plaster shoes and metal chain 150 (diameter) x 350 cm (inflated)

F 1980

● Finland

consists of a series of balloons with dark rings applied to them to remind us of women's breasts. During the exhibition the balloons slowly deflate; they were not made to retain their shape. This limited sustainability refers to the way many women experience their bodies. So *Intimately Social 4.09* has no more of a premium on eternal life than our youth or our vanity. With a bit of humour Minna Palmqvist attempts to point this out to the public.

A *Intimately Social 4.09*, 2009.
Photography: Anna Rönnqvist

Antoine Peters

1981

M

● The Netherlands

Antoine Peters (1981, Vorden, the Netherlands) graduated cum laude from the ArtEZ Institute of the Arts in Arnhem in 2004 and continued his fashion education with a master's degree from the Fashion Institute Arnhem. Even as a student Peters had begun to develop his signature style: surrealistic graphic prints that often bore a positive message about serious matters. His collections are always based on modern wardrobe classics such as jeans, the T-shirt and the sweater. His project *A sweater for the world!* from 2006 is a typical example. Peters designed a large sweater for two persons in order to bring two different people together. Besides designing for his own label, Antoine Peters has also worked for GSUS and the Effio sock label.

www.antoinepeters.com

Exhibition
— *Looong Sleeve*
2014
100% cotton
c. 30 × 1 × 1 m

A

For his collection for the spring of 2014, *Ceci n'est pas un sweater*, fashion designer Antoine Peters made a sweater with the longest sleeves in the world. The sweater was displayed in the window of the Kiki Niesten boutique in Maastricht. Peters used the sleeves to build an installation that filled the entire window, and he submitted the sweater – with sleeves more than thirty metres long – to be considered for inclusion in the Guinness Book of Records.

Like the other pieces in the collection *Ceci n'est pas un sweater*, the sweater with the longest sleeves is made of grey cotton jersey, a material that is frequently featured in almost every collection by Antoine Peters. For this spring collection, Peters turned to

the surrealistic artist René Magritte for inspiration. The collection consists of sweater dresses and unisex sweaters made of jersey, sweatshirt fabric and satin. The sweaters can be worn in so many ways that they far exceed the definition of a sweater. The goal of Antoine Peters was to make an elegant one-size-fits-all outfit that would blur the borders between daytime and evening wear.

Besides working on his collections Antoine Peters also takes on special assignments. There's something surrealistic about the look of these pieces, too, such as the dress that Peters designed in 2013 for the Museum of the Image (MOTI) in Breda. Seen from one angle this *Lenticular Dress* is a polka dot dress, and from another angle it's a dress

B

C

with stripes. Peters used traditional pleating to create this optical illusion. With this playfulness, the surrealistic quality and the 'nothing is what it seems' feeling that you get, the work of Antoine Peters continues to catch us by surprise.

A *Looong Sleeve*, 2014.
   Photography: Marc Deurloo
B *Looong Sleeve*, 2014.
   Digital sketch
C *Lenticular Dress*, 2013.
   Photography: Marc Deurloo

B

Pyuupiru

In the work of the Japanese transgender artist Pyuupiru (1974, Tokyo, Japan), her own body is always the point of departure. She began her career in the club scene: in the late nineties she made wild, extravagant costumes. As the years passed she used different media to tell her story. In a series of photographs, for example, Pyuupiru recorded her transformation from man to woman. This transformation is also recorded in the documentary *Pyuupiru 2001-2008*. The tension between being a creator on the one hand and being your own creation on the other is dealt with there as well. The film had its première at the International Film Festival in Rotterdam. *Mercury* was shown in early 2011 at Museum Boijmans Van Beuningen as part of Han Nefkens Fashion on the Edge.

1974

F

■ Japan

www.pyuupiru.com

Exhibition
— *Mercury*, from the series
  Planetaria
  2001
  Hand-knitted, urethane yarn,
  urethane, wood, iron, FRP
  c. 206 × 172 × 118 cm
  Collection of Museum Boijmans
  Van Beuningen, Rotterdam,
  loaned by Han Nefkens Fashion
  on the Edge, 2010

The Japanese artist Pyuupiru calls her extensive, transdisciplinary way of working a 'Supermacrocosm'. From make-up artist to model, from photographer and filmmaker to performance artist, Pyuupiru is a total artist who draws no borders between work and private life. 'My works are entwined with my life, but in an effort to avoid becoming too self-absorbed I try to drape them in a metaphorical "veil of beauty".' This veil of beauty, according to Pyuupiru, is also a way of stimulating the public and making her work universally accessible.

Mercury (2008) is part of the series *Planetaria*, a series of nine knitted costumes. Each of the costumes represents a planet and is designed to cover the whole body. All nine pieces were knit by Pyuupiru herself – by hand and without a knitting pattern. Each object developed in an organic way during the knitting process. For the completion of *Planetaria*, Pyuupiru gave each of the nine knitted costumes a name and a character by putting the object on and photographing herself in it. While posing, Pyuupiru gave each 'planet' its own facial expression and its own system of locomo-

tion, and she used the costumes to reinterpret herself as a human being.

Speaking of reinterpretation and transformation, a recurring theme in her work, Pyuupiru says, 'For me, the body is like a vase made of fragile glass. Liquid is an emotion of various colours poured in the vase, and identity is a will to make one pour the liquid into it. You know that the glass changes its shape when heat is added. And you know you choose what you wear by your will.'[1] Pyuupiru had her demons to wrestle with in the past, particularly the incomprehension she met with when she discovered she was a prisoner in the wrong body, but thanks to her art she found a way to experience again and again her transformation from man to woman – indeed, her transformation from death to life. Thus time after time she undergoes her rebirth, creating her own ideal 'self'.

1 See www.peril.com.au/back-editions/edition08/
   interview-with-pyuupiru/

A *Mercury*, from the
   series *Planetaria*, 2001.
   Photography: Masayuki
   Yoshinaga
B *Mercury*, from the series
   Planetaria, photographed
   in 2008

Ana Rajcevic

1983

F

● Serbia

The Serbian Ana Rajcevic (1983, Belgrade, Serbia) graduated from the London College of Fashion in 2012 with a master's degree in Fashion Artefacts. With her graduation project, *Animal – The Other Side of Evolution*, she won the 2012 London College of Fashion Design Award and the ITS Accessories Collection of the Year. Rajcevic does not call herself a fashion designer but a fashion artist. Her work lies on the border between fashion and sculpture. She prefers to work with materials such as synthetic polymers, metal and leather. She also likes working with film. In 2010 she produced the short fashion film *Encounters*, which was shown at the Rotterdam International Film Festival in 2011.

www.anarajcevic.com

Exhibition
— *Animal – The Other Side of Evolution*
  2012
  Fibreglass, polyester resin, rubber
  85 × 37 × 39 cm

Animal – The Other Side of Evolution (2012) is Ana Rajcevic's visual interpretation of the anatomy of animals. Rajcevic builds on existing skeletal structures. For the object that is being exhibited in *The Future of Fashion is Now*, Rajcevic found inspiration in the impressive form of the sting ray, using it as a point of departure for new, natural-looking sculptural structures that exude power and sensuality. To do this she explored ideas about mutation and evolution in order to arrive at a cross between man and animal and to create an image that transcends past and future. Thus she departs from the traditional context of accessories and jewellery and makes a new genre of objects that can be presented not only as sculpture but also as fashion, to be worn on the body. For her research she spent a whole year, day in and day out, at the Natural History Museum in London, where she studied the anatomy and bone structures of animals. 'It's all about boundaries in humans and animals. I like playing with the idea that we are not animals or maybe that we are. I prefer questioning within my work than coming up with answers.'[1]

Ana Rajcevic's interest in the way accessories and jewellery relate to the anatomy of the body can also be seen in earlier designs. For *Wired* (2009) she created five sculptures that examine the relationship between industrial objects and the body. She took apart ready-made objects such as mannequins and ran metal wires through them as a reference to the human body's network of blood vessels. The focus here is also on the anatomy of the body and on the question of what can be found beneath the body's surface. With *Blind Nude* (2012), Ana Rajcevic exposes the objectification of the female body by presenting to the public one of the most sensual and visible parts of a woman's body – the lips – and doing it in a new way. *Blind Nude* is a life-sized replica of Rajcevic's own lips, made from brass. She uses her lips as a form of self-objectification: while a woman's lips are seen as an instrument of sexual pleasure, Rajcevic transforms them into a frozen artefact that cannot be penetrated, either from the inside or from the outside.

1   See www.sleek-mag.com/mb/2013/09/sleek-x-mb-by-mercedes-benz-meeting-ana-rajcevic/

A

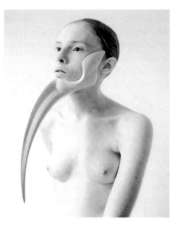

B

A-B-C-D
  Animal – The Other Side of Evolution, 2012.
  Model: Anna Tatton.
  Photography: Fernando Lessa

C

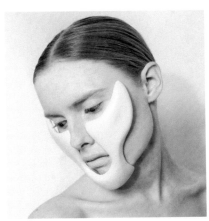

D

Craig Green

1986

M

■ United Kingdom

Craig Green (1986, London, United Kingdom) graduated from Central Saint Martins in London in 2012 with a master's degree in Fashion & Textiles. With his graduation collection, a combination of digital tie-dye prints and wooden and papier-mâché sculptures, Craig Green won the L'Oréal Professional Creative Award. Earlier, in 2010, he won the New Era XC Competition and a shoe design contest held by Bally in collaboration with Central Saint Martins. His work has also been shown in the exhibition *Arrrgh! Monsters in Fashion* in Athens, Paris and Utrecht.

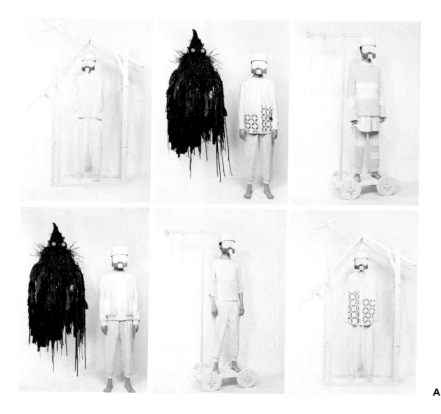

A

Craig Green grew up in North London in a family that had little affinity with fashion. With a plumber as a father and a carpenter as an uncle, Green was always surrounded by building materials, and he became fascinated by handiwork, materials and structures at an early age. Until he arrived at Central Saint Martins, Craig Green had no interest in fashion. He went to the academy with the idea of becoming a painter or sculptor. Green started the foundation course, an orientation year, but he soon realised that handiwork, materials and structures are essential aspects of fashion. So he completed his study as a fashion designer. In every collection that Craig Green designs he is guided by these three concepts. Green has a preference for cheap materials, which he then subjects to intensive artisanal treatment: 'I'm drawn to making something out of nothing, or very little. You get the cheapest materials and use your skill to make it expensive.'[1] One of Green's favourite places for gaining inspiration is the B&Q, a British do-it-yourself store.

Craig Green's background in textile and design leaves its mark on all his collections. Almost every fabric is treated by hand by him and his studio (Green is a fierce advocate of a non-digital approach), and his collection for the spring/ summer of 2013 is no exception. All the materials used in the fifteen designs that comprise the collection have been

A Presentation of spring/
   summer collection 2013.
   Photography: Fashion East
B *Look 17*, autumn/winter
   2014-2015.
   Photography: Fashion East
C *Look 18*,
   spring/summer 2014.
   Photography: Fashion East

c

intensively hand-processed. The colours are sober – ivory and black – but the material is rich: the calico, cotton, silk-screened suede and muslin in this collection have all been finished in an unusual way, with roughly trimmed anti-fray edges, stencilled buttonholes or sleeves dipped in rubber.

Not only are Craig Green's designs produced in an artisanal manner, but they can also be recognised by the recurring theme of 'boyhood fantasy', as Green himself calls it. Fashion, he believes, must be a kind of escapism. That's why all his designs contain elements of fantasy and adventure. These he unleashes on such male archetypes as the sportsman, the nomad, the religious believer and the labourer. For his autumn/winter collection for 2014-2015, Green turned to Persian carpets and the functional elements of workmen's clothing for his inspiration. 'Utilitarian for the romantic generation', as he himself describes it. In this collection, too, all the fabrics were dyed by hand and then washed until they acquired the appearance of a slightly worn Persian carpet. These hand-dyed fabrics are also central to the installation that is part of *The Future of Fashion is Now*.

1   See www.stylesalvage.blogspot.nl/2014/01/the-rise-of-craig-green.html

Look 14
installation, 2014

In this installation, Craig Green elaborates on the autumn/winter 2014-2015 men's collection, which was inspired by Persian carpets and combines working clothes with romantic elements. The installation is based on the prints and on one specific outfit from the collection. That outfit consists of several layers: a hand-dyed skirt, shirt, blouse, floor-length coat and leather harness. The coat was inspired by the Japanese *noragis*, a coat worn by labourers. The powerful, impressive silhouette is softened by the romantic print. This print, with its psychedelic colours, was made in collaboration with textile designer Helen Price.

In the installation, the outfit is shown between two screens containing hand-dyed cloths that feature the same print as the clothing and hang in the screens like carpets.

The printing technique was inspired by the *Nantong blue calico* printing and dyeing technique that was developed during the Chinese Qing Dynasty (1644-1912). During this period, the *calico*, a heavy, unfinished type of cotton, was printed with blue and white patterns in the city of Nantong, north of the Yangtze River. It was worn mainly by local farmers and fishermen, who developed the prints for their clothing based on animal and plant motifs that were taken from local Chinese folklore and expressed their desire for a good future life.

A number of craftspeople were involved in this assignment, people specialised in this highly labour-intensive blue *calico* technique. A pattern was drawn on the *calico* by hand, layer by layer, in different colours. The cloth must be dried after each colour application before the next one can be placed over it. The many layers of dye make the *calico* very stiff.

Hanka van der Voet

A-B-C
Production hand-made prints.
Photography: Craig Green
D   *Look 14*, autumn/winter
2014-2015
E   Sketch of the installation, 2014

A

The idea behind the material and painting process was to do something in reaction to how digitalised and easily reproducible textiles and prints have become in recent years. The process was a return to the way prints and textiles used to be produced. All the component parts within the piece are individually hand-painted, so each piece of cloth is a one off kind of textile. The process of the textile is a layered circular motif built up to look almost like a lap rug or stained glass window.

The commissioned piece is taken from our autumn/ winter 2014 collection. We then made the garment into an installation style piece using two of the original hand-painted rugs as hangings within the space.

The silhouettes of the autumn/winter 2014 collection that the piece is taken from are all based on heavily layered religious, almost robe-like ways of dressing. The pieces themselves act almost as vestments for the wearer.

Craig Green

B

D

New Values and
New Stories

José Teunissen

What determines the value of a fashion product and what role does the personal background of the designer play in that process? Today's designers are trying to redefine and recalibrate the fashion system in a number of ways. The leading pioneers in this area are Viktor&Rolf (the Netherlands), who have been commenting on the fashion system and exposing its hypocrisy since they began collaborating twenty years ago. With their 2013 couture show *Zen Garden* they raised the question of fashion's rapid turnover rate and its lack of spirituality. Twenty models (one for every year of their collaboration in the fashion world) paraded down a catwalk that was designed to resemble a Zen garden. Each model was then placed in position by Viktor&Rolf – who themselves were dressed as Zen masters – and arranged with the other models to form a block of stones. It was fashion 'captured in time' in an installation with eternal value, by which Viktor&Rolf put the fleeting, ephemeral character of the fashion system on the agenda. In 2012 the conceptual fashion designer Christophe Coppens (Belgium) decided to terminate his fashion career because he, too, found the system too rapid and restrictive. He incorporated his archive, collections and personal belongings into the installation *Everything is Local: Landscape Part 1* (2012-2013), thereby transforming his own fashion history into a fantasy world of recycled stuff. He used ceramics as a new expressive material and made all kinds of structures with it. In doing so he visualised how in the design process he could literally escape the restrictions and demands of the fashion system.

The designers of the new generation are quick to criticise the fashion system, the compulsion to engage in over-consumption, and concepts such as brand identity and local identity, but they are also imparting fashion with a new set of values. One important example of this is the *slow fashion* movement, whose goal is to render the fashion production system more transparent by using as many local materials as possible and by setting up a circular economy with direct lines running from producer to consumer.[1] In this movement it is essential that the fashion product itself acquires a new, sustainable *value* so that its life extends beyond that of a single season.[2] This can be done by giving fashion a new story to tell as a counterpart to the traditional 'slick' fashion campaigns that delude the consumer with a dream world. For this reason the stories in the work of many young designers often emphasise the tangibility and authenticity of the product: they focus on the materiality, experience and origin of

Slow and Steady Wins the Race – Mary Ping, *Clear* collection, 2011

the objects. The construction or creation process is very often part of the story, with Mary Ping's American label Slow and Steady Wins the Race as a fine example. Ping's aim is to demonstrate the process of every sustainable product she develops, which she does by organising exhibitions that show that her products possess a palpable, authentic value that does not refer to a glorious dream world. The materiality and the expressiveness of the fabric is also important to minä perhonen, the label of the Japanese designer Akira Minagawa. He bases his designs, fabrics and patterns on forms from nature, which he draws by hand and then develops. In many of his fabrics he combines an extraordinary artisanal approach with new technologies. His poetic fabrics can be used in clothing as well as in furniture and interiors. He deliberately tries to escape from the ephemerality of fashion by using his fabrics and designs over and over again and to work them into extremely simple, classical dresses, skirts and jackets that are rarely subject to fashion trends. In her project *Made by Rain* (2012), Aliki van der Kruijs (the Netherlands) lets the material speak for itself. She designs shawls from indigo that she lays outside on her roof, where she lets the rain showers determine the design. Each shawl comes with a folder that tells when the rain fell and how heavy it was.

The importance of maintaining a more sustainable relationship with the things we surround ourselves with is emphasised by Little Shilpa (India), who collects discarded items and gives them a second life as new outfits. She focuses her attention on the 'artisanal' quality of an object and the energy it cost to make it, exposing the development of the consumer society in the fashion world.

In his project *The Welsh Space Campaign* (2013) interdisciplinary artist and designer Hefin Jones (United Kingdom) asks what kind of impact

Little Shilpa – Shilpa Chavan, *Headonism*, 2009

old crafts and local traditions could have on the future of the fashion system. He engaged local craftsmen from Wales to make a woollen spacesuit, thereby drawing attention to the importance and power of local and traditional craftsmanship for the future.

In addition to this focus on the power and reassessment of craftsmanship, there are also more theoretical approaches to discussing fashion as a system. Fashion designer Adele Varcoe (Australia) is conducting a PhD study on the relationship between fashion, body and identity by holding performances in public spaces and studying their effects. In 2012 she presented the performance *Imagining Chanel* in which she brought a Chanel fashion show from the 1920s to life by using the original texts and model poses from that period. The models on the catwalk were naked, however, just as in the fairy tale *The Emperor's New Clothes*. In this way the public discovered that the Chanel brand is recognisable even when there are no actual clothes to look at. The ironic conclusion that can be drawn is that the identity of the brand is stronger than that of the clothing product itself. In the work *11″ x 17″* by Elisa van Joolen (the Netherlands), the effect of the fashion brand is clarified and criticised in yet another way.

What these designers are not interested in is the dream world of magic and glamour that is usually served up by the big fashion brands, fashion shows and fashion magazines. They train their sights on the tangible, concrete dimension of fashion, emphasising its artisanal power and embracing its timeless, sustainable aspects.

1   The aim here is comparable to that of the slow food movement.
2   Hazel Clark, 'Slow + Fashion: An Oxymoron – or a Promise for the Future..?',
    in: Jan Brand and José Teunissen (eds.), *A Fashion Odyssey: Progress in Fashion and Sustainability*, Arnhem 2013, pp. 108-130.

Viktor&Rolf
Viktor Horsting and Rolf Snoeren

M + M   1969

The Netherlands

Even back in their school days at the Arnhem Institute of the Arts (the predecessor of the ArtEZ Institute of the Arts), Viktor Horsting (1969, Geldrop, the Netherlands) and Rolf Snoeren (1969, Dongen, the Netherlands) worked together. After graduating in 1992 they left for Paris. One year later they won first prize from the prestigious Salon Européen des Jeunes Créateurs in Hyères and their reputation was secure. With their experimental designs and installations they passed sharp criticism on the fashion world, especially on its commercial outgrowths. Yet they themselves became more and more a part of that world: in 1998 they showed their first couture collection, in 2000 their first prêt-à-porter collection, in 2003 their first menswear collection and in 2005 they launched their first perfume: *Flowerbomb*. But judging from the concept and creations of *Zen Garden*, their drive to innovate is far from being depleted.

www.viktor-rolf.com

Exhibition
— *Zen Garden*, group 1 to 9
  Haute couture collection,
  autumn/winter 2013-2014
  Collection of Museum Boijmans
  Van Beuningen, Rotterdam,
  donated by Han Nefkens
  Fashion on the Edge, 2013
— *Red Carpet*
  Haute couture collection,
  autumn/winter 2014-2015
  Collection of Han Nefkens
  Fashion on the Edge, 2014

With the collection *Zen Garden* (autumn/winter 2013), Viktor&Rolf returned to the world of haute couture after a respite of thirteen years. There was something surprising about that long absence, given the fact that the designers have always declared their affection for haute couture in interviews. Mainly this had to do with couture's possibilities for experimentation, which of course is always more difficult in prêt-à-porter collections.

Zen Garden can be seen as a summary, perhaps even as the essence of twenty years of Viktor&Rolf. The couture show began in complete darkness with the designers seated back-to-back in the middle of the podium and lit by a single spotlight, as if deep in meditation. Finally they stood up, and it was only then that the lights went on and the space was suddenly unveiled. The floor of the podium had been covered with sand that had been carefully raked in a circular pattern, inspired by the famous rock garden of the Ryoan-ji temple in Kyoto. Accompanied by subdued music, which only seemed to heighten the silence and contemplative atmosphere, the models came out one by one. Twenty different models in twenty different outfits, one model for each year of the fashion house's existence, and all dressed in what at first glance appeared to be sober and simple creations in black artificial silk. This monochrome colour scheme was quite deliberate, of course, since it allowed all the attention to be focused on the silhouettes and constructions without being diverted by colours and materials. And this is what Viktor&Rolf have always been after: these constructions, these innovative silhouettes. As if to emphasise this, the two themselves were also constantly present on the podium, adding last-minute finishing touches to the clothing. The models then gathered together in small groups – sitting, lying – with the wide fabric of their dresses and capes being carefully arranged by the designers. When all was finished, the models seemed to have been transformed into dark masses of rock, owing to the black of the fabric and the designs, which had been made to achieve just this effect. They had become part of the Zen garden. Fashion, whose rapid changes and transience have often been commented on by Viktor&Rolf, was brought to a standstill here and rendered eternal.

Art collector Han Nefkens, who in 2009 commissioned Viktor&Rolf to make a work for the exhibition *The Art of Fashion*, acquired ten of the twenty designs from *Zen Garden* for his initiative Han Nefkens Fashion on the Edge.

A   *Zen Garden*, presentation
    haute couture collection, 2013.
    Photography: © Team Peter
    Stigter

A

Christophe Coppens

Christophe Coppens (1969, Sint Niklaas, Belgium) was trained as an actor and film director, but after graduating he devoted himself to fashion, hats and accessories, under his own name and for other designers. After his first experimental collection in 1990 Coppens quickly made a name for himself and produced hats for Issey Miyake and Guy Laroche, among others. Pop stars such as Rihanna, Grace Jones and Roïsin Murphy also asked him for special designs, as did the Belgian Royal Family. His label was sold in more than 140 shops worldwide. In 2012 he decided to shut his business down. Since then he has worked on installations and exhibitions as a self-employed artist.

www.christophecoppens.com

Exhibition
— *Well not for me:*
  Landscape 1+2=3
  2012-2014
  Installation: mixed media
  Landscape Part 1: Collection
  of Museum Boijmans Van Beuningen, Rotterdam, loaned by
  Han Nefkens Fashion on the
  Edge, 2013
  Landscape Part 2: Collection
  Christophe Coppens

In May 2012 Christophe Coppens closed down his business and studio. After working for 21 years as a successful designer of fashion, hats and accessories, then as a maker of installations on the cutting edge of fashion and art, he decided to get off the treadmill that is such an unavoidable part of running a fashion business. In the bankruptcy that followed, the receiver came and went, leaving him with nothing. His status, his money, his studio and – according to Coppens – even his identity were gone. Yet looking back, the bankruptcy just may have been a blessing in disguise. For years Coppens had been toying with the idea of working as a full-time artist, but he had always held off on account of his commercial context as a designer. Now he had the chance to devote himself entirely to art.

Ceramics had always been his great love, and just before the bankruptcy Coppens

A

had begun studying with the ceramic artist Hugo Meert. One of the first works he made there was a mountain, soon to be followed by about three hundred more. The mountain turned out to be the perfect form for processing the trauma and distress associated with the loss of his business. He could incorporate everything into it that reminded him of his former life and identity. What that meant first of all was his clothes, often made by fellow designers such as Dries Van Noten and Martin Margiela. The clothes no longer fit him, figuratively speaking. They belonged to his former life, and Coppens decided to cut them all up and process them into works of art. He did the same thing with his sketch books, his archive, his photographs and his folders of clippings. Literally everything that belonged to his former professional identity had to be destroyed to make room for a new future. A few months later, during a visit to friends in Los Angeles, the future took on a different dimension. Coppens was profoundly struck by the

climate of Los Angeles, by the colours and the light, but mainly by the mountains that surround the city. He immediately felt at home and decided on the spot to move there. Now he could chop up what remained of his furniture and household goods, and this, too, was converted into mountains.

An important pillar of strength for Coppens's redefinition of himself was Han Nefkens. Coppens had called the patron and art collector, who had commissioned work from him on more than one occasion, to tell him about the upcoming bankruptcy. Nefkens called him the next day to commission something new. 'Make whatever you want,' he had said. And so *Everything is Local, Landscape Part 1* came into being. *Landscape Part 2* and *Well not for me: Landscape 1+2=3* would soon follow.

A-B Exhibition *Everything is Local, Landscape Part 1* in Museum Boijmans Van Beuningen, 2013. Photography: Lotte Stekelenburg
C *Everything is Local, Landscape Part 2*, 2013. Photography: Koji Fujii

B

c

Nuages Gris
Jeroen Teunissen and Dorith Sjardijn

1974 + 1983

M + F

● The Netherlands

Jeroen Teunissen (1974, Valkenswaard, the Netherlands) studied autonomous art at the ArtEZ Institute of the Arts in Arnhem and went on to earn his master's degree at the same institute. He and Melanie Rozema had their own label for a few years. He also worked as chief menswear designer at Viktor&Rolf, did styling and design assignments for De Bijenkorf and G-Star, and has been teaching at ArtEZ since 2009. His work has been shown in Rome, Paris, Tokyo and New York, among other places, as well as in the Netherlands.

Dorith Sjardijn (1983, The Hague, the Netherlands) studied textile and fashion at the Royal Academy of Art in The Hague, where she specialised in smart textiles. In 2009 she was one of the initiators and then curator of the travelling exhibition *Pretty Smart Textiles*, which was shown in the Netherlands, Austria, Denmark and Belgium. Sjardijn develops collections for different fashion brands and also teaches at the Royal Academy of Art in The Hague and the Maastricht Academy of Fine Arts and Design.

www.nuagesgris.com

Exhibition
— *Objet trouvé*
2014
Fabric, printed PCB

A Sketch: *dematerialised fashion manifested as artistic vision*, 2014
B *Objet trouvé*, 2014. Photography: Lonneke van der Palen

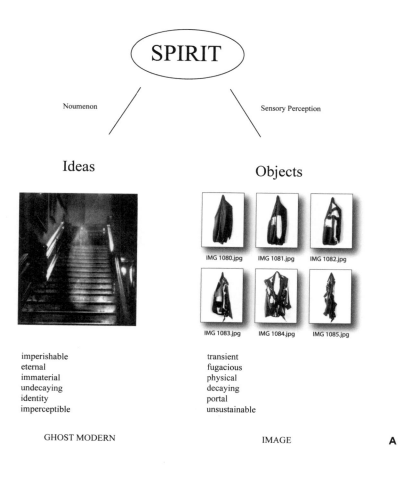

SPIRIT

Noumenon   Sensory Perception

Ideas   Objects

IMG 1080.jpg   IMG 1081.jpg   IMG 1082.jpg

IMG 1083.jpg   IMG 1084.jpg   IMG 1085.jpg

imperishable   transient
eternal   fugacious
immaterial   physical
undecaying   decaying
identity   portal
imperceptible   unsustainable

GHOST MODERN   IMAGE   A

In his search for the essence of fashion, fashion designer Helmut Lang introduced the so-called *accessoires vêtements* in 1997: elements of garments that he regarded as critical to his style and that, even when stripped of all the fabric around them, still clearly conveyed his signature and identified the garment as a real 'Helmut Lang'. With shirts, for example, it had to do with the collar, the yoke, the placket front and the hem. Nuages Gris have chosen these *accessoires vêtements* as the point of departure for their project *Objet trouvé*, a title whose reference to the conceptual art of Marcel Duchamp is certainly not accidental. Just as Duchamp gave his famous urinal new meaning by elevating it to a work of art, so Nuages Gris applies a contemporary interpretation of Lang's original idea to the *accessoires vêtements*. The designers do this by coming up with a reinterpretation of 'smart textile', in this case a conductive material that converts movement into data that can then be sent on to a microprocessor. With this data they create a new digital fashion identity.

But *Objet trouvé* isn't just an installation. It's also a research project. By introducing these kinds of sensors into articles of clothing, Nuages Gris would make it possible to charge a garment with meaning whenever it is worn. A sensor would be able to register movements, for example, enabling it to tell us something about the wearer. It could register states of mind as well. Or pinpoint the wearer's location. Such sensors in clothing could also be useful in the future for creating 'augmented reality' by adding an extra layer of meaning. Thus an article of clothing would function like today's mobile telephone, which is no longer a device for simply making phone calls. The longer we have the phone the more information it accumulates and the more it becomes part of our identity. While an article of clothing usually begins losing value the moment we buy it, in this way it would constantly increase in value.

B

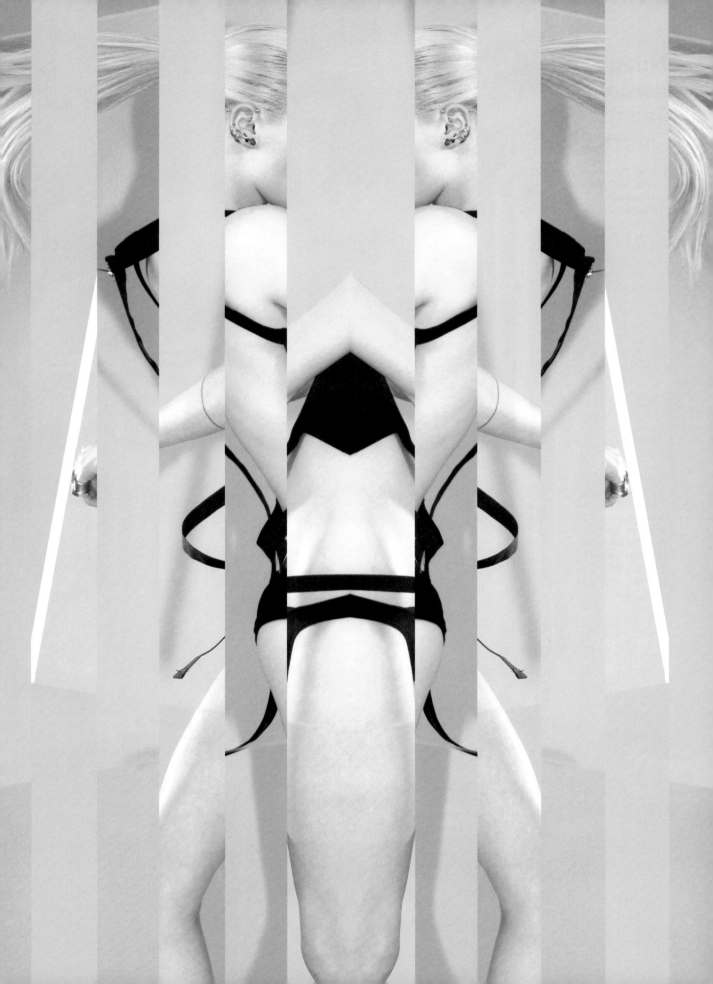

What do old crafts and local traditions mean for our modern age? Or for the future, for that matter? That's the question underlying *The Welsh Space Campaign*, a project created by interdisciplinary artist and designer Hefin Jones.

Once Wales had a flourishing wool industry, but now, like so many other crafts and small-scale industries, it's practically disappeared. As part of his graduation project at Goldsmiths College, University of London, Wales, Jones began searching for the country's last remaining wool mills and asked the few craftsmen who were still working there to help him make an astronaut's suit. He wasn't so much interested in making an astronaut's suit as such but in creating a cosmic environment for the Welsh culture, skills and traditions. In doing so, he hoped to raise the craftsmen's ambitions and silent dreams to a very different level, to invite them to think about the use of local crafts and skills in a place as far away from them as possible: outer space. This was a project that called for a good dose of chauvinism. Jones's ultimate goal was 'to reveal that Wales has the capacity to explore space, and to show that off-world-culturalisation can be achieved through a collective communitarian effort'. So everything needed for the project was made by local craftsmen in Wales. The fabric for the suit was made by a wool mill, the pressure system in the suit – essential for staying alive in space – was made by an old-fashioned plumber, and the space clogs were made by a traditional clog maker. Even the emblem of the space mission has a Welsh connotation: the upward-pointing red arrow is actually the end of the tail of the dragon that is pictured on the Welsh flag.

Earning his bachelor's degree did not mean the end of the project for Hefin Jones. In collaboration with physicists from Aberystwyth University he is thinking about ways to send Welsh cultural objects into space. He is also working with the poet Ceri Wyn Jones on a poem about counting down from ten to one, in which each number refers to a different aspect of Welsh culture.

Hefin Jones

Hefin Jones (1991, Haverfordwest, United Kingdom) studied Design & Technology at Cardigan Secondary School from 2002 to 2009, and Arts & Design at the West Wales School of the Arts in Carmarthen, Wales, from 2009 to 2010. In 2013 he graduated summa cum laude with a bachelor's degree from Goldsmiths College, University of London. For his graduation project *The Welsh Space Campaign* he received the Christine Risley Award. Hefin Jones lives and works in London.

www.hefinjones.co.uk
www.welshspacecampaign.com
www.vimeo.com/67436669

1991

M

● United Kingdom

Exhibition
— *The Welsh Space Campaign*
  2013
  Spacesuit, flag and video
  200 × 100 × 100 cm

B

A-B *The Welsh Space Campaign*, 2013.
Photography: Dan Burn-Forti

Elisa van Joolen

1983

F

The Netherlands

Elisa van Joolen (1983, The Hague, the Netherlands) graduated cum laude from the Gerrit Rietveld Academy in Amsterdam in 2006. With the support of study grants from the Queen Sophia Foundation, the Prins Bernhard Cultuurfonds and the Mondriaan Fund, among others, she continued her training in Italy, Japan and finally New York, where she completed her MFA in Fashion Design and Society at Parsons The New School for Design in 2012. Her work has been shown at exhibitions in the Netherlands, the United States, China and Japan. Elisa van Joolen teaches at the Gerrit Rietveld Academy and at the Goldsmiths College of the University of London.

Exhibition
— *11″ x 17″*
Since 2013
Series of basic-wear, made from clothes and shoes provided by various fashion labels

A

A   *11″ x 17″* sweater 'Russell Athletic x Rockwell by Parra x G-Star RAW', 2014. Photography: Blommers/Schumm
B-C-D-E
11″ x 17″, sketches

The fashion system as we know it has been under a great deal of pressure in recent years. The wasting of raw and auxiliary materials, the use of pesticides in the production of cotton, abuses in factories in low-wage countries, huge quantities of clothing that are produced but never sold: for more and more people it's clear that the fashion industry cannot go on like this, that something has to change in the way we use and produce clothing.

In her project *11″ x 17″*, Elisa van Joolen entered into a dialogue, literally and figuratively, with major brands such as G-Star, Nike, O'Neill and gsus sindustries, but also with small labels such as Rockwell by Parra, Shelley Fox and Monique van Heist. She was given many different articles of clothing and shoes from these and other brands that were unsuitable for sale: samples, overproduction, old stock, archival pieces. For Van Joolen the garments became the starting point for two new collections: one consisting of sweaters and the other of sneakers, *the* basic items of our time. She cut them into pieces and created new combinations that incorporated the materials, details and finishing from a very wide range of brands and sources, from high-end to second-hand. This combination of styles, materials and brands immediately raises questions about the origin of the garments. What is their value? Who is the maker? Who is the designer? And what is left of a recognisable brand when it is cut up and combined to form a new article of clothing?

There were many prior questions, especially from the PR people working for the companies she approached. They compelled Van Joolen to further elaborate her basic principles and ideas and to formulate them better. These conversations, mainly carried on by e-mail, were also an important part of the project for Van Joolen. The entire point of the project, was the interaction with the fashion industry, the provocative dialogue.

B

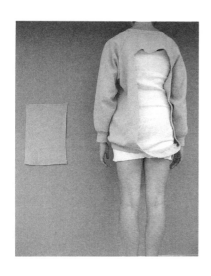

C

In Van Joolen's collection *Invert Footwear*, sneakers from major brands such as Nike and Converse are turned inside out and partially cut up to pieces. Once they have been stripped of their brand identity we are able to look at them with very different eyes. Stitched seams and materials become more prominent and emphasise the efforts of the factory worker, which normally disappear behind the label. Nor do the soles escape Van Joolen's deconstruction. She cuts them loose and replaces them with cheap flip-flops, which are sold all over the world for a couple of euros. And she takes the soles from the expensive brand-name sneakers and makes holes in them for shoelaces, transforming them into a kind of flip-flop. What is their value then? Who is their maker?

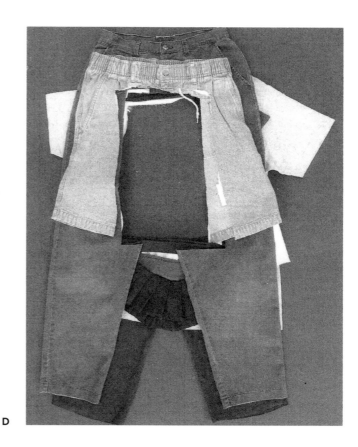

D

E

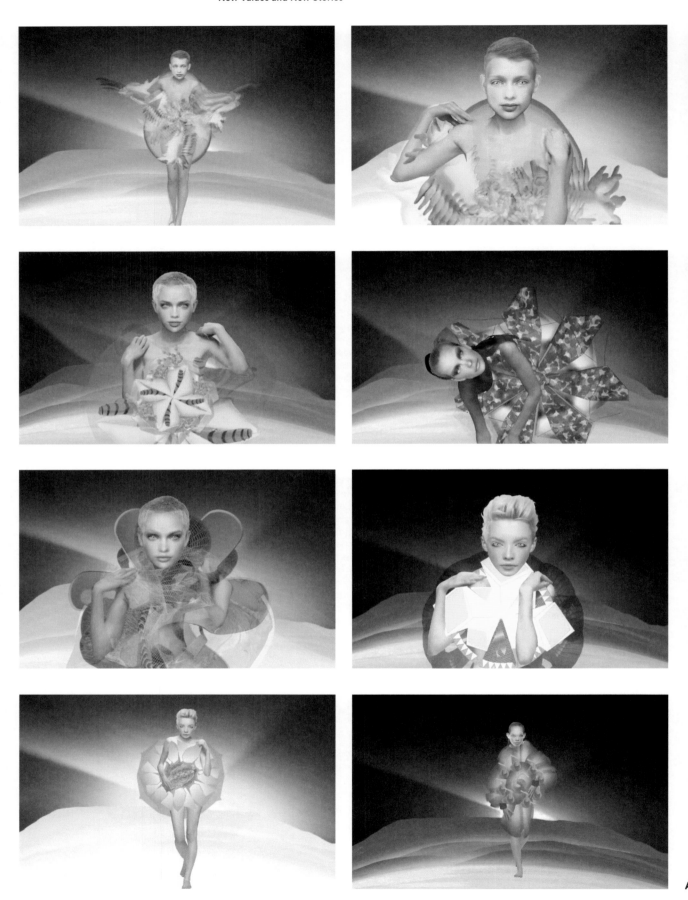

A

Jacob Kok

Jacob Kok (1979, Zwolle, the Netherlands) studied animation and audiovisual design at the Gerrit Rietveld Academy in Amsterdam and fashion at the Royal Academy of Art in The Hague. In 2011 he won the prize offered by the Dutch television programme *Project Catwalk* with his *Oerknal* collection. Two years later he began collaborating with the makers of the computer game *The Sims*, for which he designed a virtual collection. Jacob Kok lives and works in Amsterdam and teaches at the Willem de Kooning Academy in Rotterdam.

www.jacobkok.com
www.vimeo.com/57477342
www.vimeo.com/66168302

Exhibition
— *Evolution*
 2014
 Animation video

1979

M

The Netherlands

For Jacob Kok, the virtual world of computer games like *The Sims* and *Second Life* is much more interesting than the real world, especially when it comes to designing clothing. When a collection is designed for the 'real' world, there are all kinds of practical matters that must be taken into account such as wearability, production, target group and pricing. But virtual reality knows no limits: in principle anything goes. 'I see the virtual world as another reality that offers many new possibilities', says Kok. 'There are no well-beaten paths, no rules: it's a domain where fantasy is in charge.'

Trained as a maker of animated films at the Rietveld Academy in Amsterdam, Kok came to the fashion world in a roundabout way. In his first animated films there were lots of naked characters, but at a certain point he thought they ought to be wearing something. An ordinary T-shirt was simply ordinary, so his creations became more and more unusual. Finally they became so interesting that they could also serve as a 'real' collection for the real world. Suddenly he wasn't just a filmmaker anymore; he was also a fashion designer. This combining of functions is beautifully revealed in the video *Paradise AW13/14*, in which a model is shown wearing a large number of colourful, spectacular designs. At first we see her in a rapidly edited sequence of stills, revolving on a pedestal; a bit later she's striding around in what at first appears to be an empty room. As the film progresses, the living model is almost imperceptibly replaced every now and then by an animated version of herself. Reality and virtual reality flow together almost seamlessly, and this is exactly the intersection that so intrigues Jacob Kok. But as far as the clothing collection shown in the video is concerned, it was a dangerous intersection. After all, a commercial collection that is being sold supposes that certain concessions are being made to all that fantasy. The clothing must be wearable, affordable, and so forth: all practical problems that do not exist in the virtual world. Kok says that he doesn't yet know whether he's willing to make such concessions, just as he doesn't know yet whether he wants to be a filmmaker or a fashion designer. In the video *Evolution* he seems to be opting for the role of filmmaker, but maybe later on he'll become a designer in the spirit of Walter Van Beirendonck and manage to create an eccentric oeuvre out of virtual reality, just as Van Beirendonck does from the world of comic strips.

A   *Evolution*, video stills, 2014
B   *Paradise*, video still,
    autumn/winter 2013-2014

Aliki van der Kruijs

Aliki van der Kruijs (1984, Deurne, the Netherlands) studied fashion at the ArtEZ Institute of the Arts in Arnhem, did an internship under A.F. Vandevorst and Klavers van Engelen, and worked for one year at G-Star in the department of material development. In 2012 she earned a master's degree in applied arts from the Sandberg Institute in Amsterdam and started her own studio. She has also served as a guest instructor at the Gerrit Rietveld Academy in Amsterdam. She has self-published several books dealing with her projects, including *Made by Rain*. Her work is frequently exhibited in the Netherlands as well as in Berlin, Brussels and Beijing. In April 2014 her submission was part of the Holland Pavilion at the Hannover Messe.

www.alikivanderkruijs.com

The designing of clothing and fabrics is a fairly purpose-oriented occupation for most designers. They have a particular image in mind, or they start with a particular vision and work towards an end result. But not Aliki van der Kruijs. For her it's all about process, and natural elements such as the weather play a major role. You don't have to look far to explain Van der Kruijs's fascination with the weather. When her grandfather died he left her twelve calendars in which he had written down what the weather was for each day. With her work she's following in his footsteps.

Rain is a distinctive feature in the Dutch landscape, so Van der Kruijs has rain figure prominently in her textile designs. On the flat roof of her Amsterdam studio she stretches pieces of natural silk that she has prepared with a thin layer of ink, which reacts with water. Or she drapes the fabric over a chair, a trestle or a set of stairs. Then it's just a matter of waiting until it rains. The rain can fall in different forms: as drizzle, as a fresh spring shower, as a torrential downpour, as a deluge. It can fall straight down from the sky or in every direction, blown about by the wind. A wide range of patterns are formed depending on the type of rain, and they're always different. In this way Van der Kruijs produces cloths – hydrographics – that are endlessly unique. They're timeless, she says, and they never grow stale, simply because they haven't been made by human hands and steer clear of fashions and trends. She makes dresses from the fabric as well as blouses and shawls, and she carefully documents the history of each garment's development. Each one comes with a report that states where the cloth was made, at what time and in what kind of weather. The cloths are thus visual witnesses to the natural conditions.

Exhibition
— *Made by Rain*, since 2013
  Pluviagraph, silk, ink, rain.
  Patternbook, shawl, fabric
  samples. Silk prints for the
  rain cape of Elsien Gringhuis'
  autumn/winter-collection
  2013-2014
— *Colour*, since 2012
  Hydrography, silk, ink, water.
  Shawl and film documentation
  of the *Colour* production process. Silk prints for the blouse
  of Elsien Gringhuis' autumn/
  winter-collection 2013-2014

1984

F

● The Netherlands

C

A   *Made by Rain*, print of the Dutch rain on a 100% silk shawl, location: 52° 21′ 11.13″ N / 4° 54′ 21.78. 21″ E, 2013. Photography: Pim Leenen

B   *Made by Rain*, rain water printed textile, location: 52° 21′ 34.13″ N / 4° 55′ 39″ E, d.d. (from left to right):
#1: 20 april 2012
#2: 20 april 2012
#3: 5 april 2012
#4: 8 april 2012
#5: 22 and 23 april 2012

C   *Made by Rain*, production process, print of Dutch rain on cotton, location: 52° 21′ 34.13″ N / 4° 55′39″ E, 2013.

minä perhonen
Akira Minagawa

1967

M

■ Japan

Akira Minagawa (1967, Tokyo, Japan) studied at Bunka Fashion College in Tokyo and launched his own fashion label in 1995. In 2003 he gave his label the name minä perhonen (Finnish for 'I butterfly'), inspired by his affinity for modern Scandinavian design from the fifties and mainly for the Finnish architect Alvar Aalto. At first his designs were only sold in Japan, mainly in his own shops in Tokyo and Kyoto, but in 2004 he began showing his collections in Paris and the brand was available world- wide. He also designs fabrics and tableware for Kvadrat and iittala, among other companies. In 2006 Minagawa was awarded the presti- gious Japanese Mainichi Fashion Grand Prix. The Audax Textile Museum in Tilburg presented his work in 2009 at a solo exhibition.

www.mina-perhonen.jp

Exhibition
— *Forest Parade*
Hana Yuki
Since spring/summer 2005 and autumn/winter 2014-2015 Installation, mixed media (garments, fabric swatches, furniture accessories, photographs)

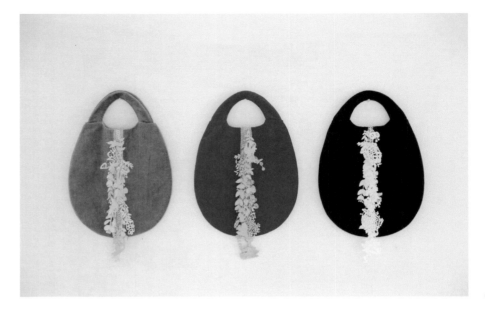

The clothing that Akira Minagawa designs for his label minä perhonen is always very simple: straight little dresses, simple waist- coats and trousers, classical blouses and shirts. They're timeless designs that are virtually impossible to date, and that's exactly what Minagawa is aiming for. They last for a very long time and have nothing to do with the big fashion circus, where a design can be worn for only one season before it's outflanked by something new. For Minagawa, artisanal handwork and craftsmanship have a higher priority, and that is expressed first of all in his fabric designs. Here nature is his main source of inspiration. Leaves, grass, birds, butterflies, flowers and even entire landscapes are restored to their essence and find their way in delicate, dreamy fabrics that effort- lessly evoke the experience of a walk in the countryside. To get as close as possible

to that experience, Minagawa works with traditional materials like pencils and brush- es. He believes that the personal hand of the designer comes closer to the irregularities of nature – to feelings and to real life – than working with a computer. Because of this there's always something sketchy about his designs, as if they had been tossed off on the spot.

With his meticulous patterns and lovely weaving techniques, Minagawa's work is rooted in both the Scandinavian and the Japanese traditions. In Japan, a great deal of attention has been paid over the centu- ries on the development and processing of fabrics, and the most ingenious techniques have been used to achieve the desired effects. An example of such a technique is Jacquard weaving. Because of its complex- ity, the Jacquard loom was almost phased out of existence, but Minagawa modernised it and adapted it for the beautiful, three- dimensional *Hana Yuki* panther motif, which involves an alternation of short and long piles that give it a very lifelike look. For *Forest Parade* he rendered forest motifs, such as leaves, flowers and birds, into a fragile lace. The three-dimensional forms that emerge are frequently featured in his collections. But despite his love for traditional tech- niques, Minagawa is not a nostalgic person or a traditionalist. Rather, he represents a new spirit of the times in which intrinsic quality is highly valued and an article of clothing is allowed to ripen over the years, absorbing more and more meaning and becoming more and more a part of the wearer's life story. Time goes on, but some values are eternal.

A *Forest Parade*,
egg-shaped bags,
autumn/winter 2013-2014.
Photography: Koji Honda
B *Hana Yuki*, panther-like coat,
autumn/winter 2014-2015.
Photography: Koji Honda
C *Forest Parade*,
original drawing,
spring/summer 2005.
Photography: L.A. Tomari

B

c

139

1974

F

■ India

Little Shilpa
Shilpa Chavan

Shilpa Chavan (1974, Mumbai, India) graduated in 1996 in Apparel Manufacture and Design as well as in Jewellery Design, both at SVDT Women's University in Mumbai. She worked for several years as a stylist for films and photo shoots, then enrolled in a summer school programme at Central Saint Martins and the London College of Fashion. At Central Saint Martins she became a qualified milliner, a skill she further perfected during an internship at Philip Treacy. Under her own brand name, Little Shilpa, she designs clothing, hats, jewellery and accessories.

Exhibition
— *Grey Matters*
(1 garment)
spring/summer 2014
Various media and techniques

A

B

The work of Shilpa Chavan the designer is influenced to a large extent by the work of Shilpa Chavan the stylist. She herself says that when designing a new piece she always thinks about how it's going to look in a photograph. And then she's always searching for objects and forms that she somehow can incorporate into the work she has in mind. Whether it's a simple flip-flop, a paper kite, toy soldiers and helicopters or old insignias, in the eclectic world of Little Shilpa anything can be used and reused to make interesting new forms and designs. And entirely in keeping with the spirit of traditional crafts, she always does everything herself, and always by hand. Chavan will have nothing to do with mass production. She makes unique pieces that are different every time, different in colour or different in details. They're often spectacular pieces that greatly appeal to artists such as Lady Gaga, but that fashion journalist Colin McDowell insists belong in a museum or gallery rather than on the catwalk.

Chavan is only too conscious of the dilemma in which she finds herself: in the art world her work is seen as conceptual fashion while the fashion world sees it as art. For Chavan herself it's all about her love of beauty and of the traditional crafts that produce that beauty but are constantly being threatened in the rush of modern life, certainly in a cosmopolitan city like Mumbai. So much is thoughtlessly thrown away, so much is dismissed as useless. Chavan wants to take those objects, which are often beautifully made, and give them a second life, and in doing so to alert people to the artisanal qualities that were needed to make them. To that end she's constantly building up collections. She never has a preconceived plan for what she collects, but always allows herself to be led by what she finds. Sometimes it takes years before she knows exactly what she's going to do with a certain object or collection. She spent seven years, for example, collecting military paraphernalia from all over the world, which finally resulted in the *Battle Royale* collection. She provided a new context for things that everyone had thrown away. Being in the collection gave them a whole new purpose, and their original beauty was restored as well. In *Grey Matters* the starting point is the sari. In this collection, too, Chavan began with a traditional Indian garment, one that is often taken for granted, and managed to revalue it by using it in a completely different context.

A *Battle Royale*,
autumn/winter 2009-2010.
Photography: Prasad Naik
B *Fleurs du mal*, 2011.
Photography: Shilpa Chavan
C *Grey Matters*,
spring/summer 2014.
Model: Erika Packard.
Photography: Prasad Naik

Slow and Steady Wins the Race
Mary Ping

1978

F

■ United States

Mary Ping (1978, New York, United States) graduated from Vassar College in Poughkeepsie, NY, in 2000 with a bachelor of fine arts degree. In 2001 she left for London, where she took classes in fashion design at the London College of Fashion and served as an intern with Robert Carey Williams. That same year she began a fashion label under her own name, which she renamed Slow and Steady Wins the Race in 2002. Her clothing and bags are now sold worldwide in a limited number of specialised shops. Slow and Steady Wins the Race also regularly makes installations for museums and galleries. In 2005 Mary Ping was one of the five winners of the Ecco Domani Fashion Foundation Award.

www.slowandsteadywinstherace.com

Exhibition
— *Clear* collection
spring/summer 2012
Mixed media

A

A   *Clear* collection,
    installation at Paul
    Rudolph Foundation, 2011.
    Photography: Isabel
    Asha Penzlien
B   *Clear* collection,
    transparent pump (green
    PVC, transparent heel),
    spring/summer 2012.
    Photography: Isabel
    Asha Penzlien
C   *Clear* collection,
    transparent shopper (suede,
    vinyl), transparent double
    cufflink, spring/summer 2012.
    Photography: Isabel
    Asha Penzlien
D   *Clear* collection,
    transparent trench coat
    (vinyl), spring/summer 2012.
    Photography: Isabel
    Asha Penzlien

No one can have failed to notice that sportswear is becoming more and more firmly entrenched in the fashion scene. The trend has made its way over from the United States – New York in particular. Even in the years following the Second World War, New Yorkers loved clothing that was presentable enough for the office but could also easily be worn while negotiating the busy city streets. The clothing from Slow and Steady Wins the Race is part of that tradition of multi-layered, easy combinations for daytime wear and not overly formal clothing for the evening.

Mary Ping, the designer behind Slow and Steady, was born and raised in New York but has a Chinese background. Her sense of style was nourished by the elegant wardrobes of her mother and grandmother but was also influenced by the streets of Queens. Fashion has to look good in terms of design, according to Mary Ping, but it also has to be accessible to everyone. Expensive, luxurious materials pose an impediment to this idea, which is why she doesn't use them. She also rejects the commerce-driven, rapid succession of collections, as a result of which barely worn clothing quickly falls out of fashion. She prefers to issue timeless collections that are not dictated by seasons, using materials that everyone can afford. 'The work is a logical dissection of fashion, an investigation into the basic elements of what we wear, and a considered response to the hyper-consumerist

B

C

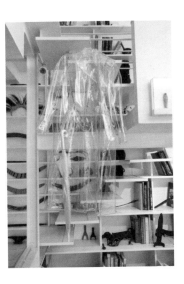

D

pace of fashion.' So for the third collection of Slow and Steady Wins the Race she turned her attention to the handbag. For most big brands the handbag is a money spinner: it's a favourite status symbol, executed in the most luxurious materials and sold at exorbitant prices – which makes it unattainable for most women. Ping decided to imitate these iconic bags. She retained the form but left out the exclusive leathers and gold fittings, opting instead for cheap canvas and equally cheap fasteners from the corner hardware store. And what happened? The bags were immediately recognised as having been inspired by designs by Chanel, Dior, Gucci, Balenciaga and other luxury labels. The designs held up, even without their expen-

sive materials, and for Ping that was proof that in fashion it's not all about expensive materials but about interesting designs made from simple fabrics.

In the *Clear* collection she reduced the design to its essence in yet another way. She made transparent versions of classical styles from the Slow and Steady catalogue: trench coats, shoes, bags and accessories made of glass and translucent plastic. Beauty reduced to the form and honesty of transparent material.

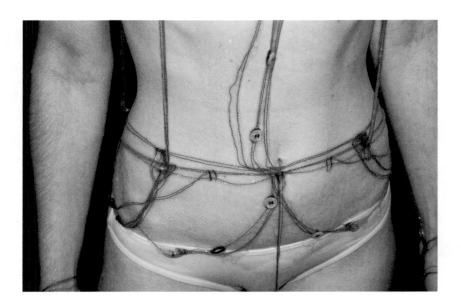

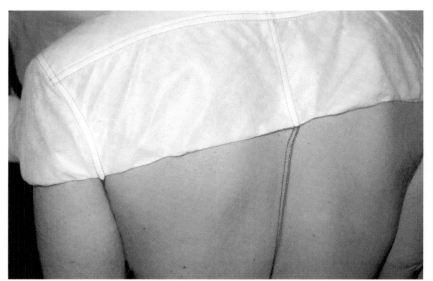

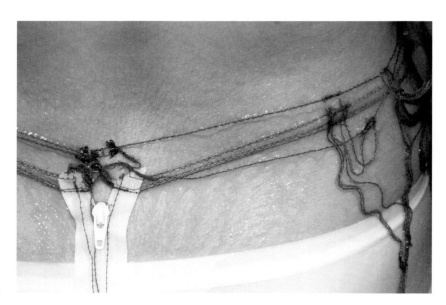

A

B

At first it seemed as if Lara Torres was about to make a brilliant career for herself in the standard fashion industry. After having graduated as a fashion designer from the Centro de Formação Profissional do Têxtil e do Vestuário (CITEX) in Porto in 2004, she won the first prize that same year at the Sangue Novo, the platform for young designers in Lisbon. The prize consisted of an internship with Alexander McQueen in London. Back in Portugal she was asked to become a junior designer at Miguel Rios Design Studio, where she mainly focused on 'intelligent' clothing and fashion technology. But the longer she worked in the fashion world the more questions she had: about working as a designer, about the function of clothing and fashion, about the relationship between clothing and identity, about the transitory nature of fashion. And particularly about the relationship between clothing and memory. She became convinced that she did not want to become an ordinary clothing designer. Rather, she wanted to approach fashion from a theoretical, artistic and investigative point of view. And it also quickly became clear that she wanted to draw other elements into her work such as films, photography, ceramics and jewellery. The result was the 2007 project *Mimesis II ī Fac Simile*, which included a kind of fashion show in which the models undressed themselves and each other slowly and provocatively as a comment on the transience and speed of the regular shows during the Lisbon Fashion Week, which was being held at the same time. In this project she also experimented with garments made from porcelain, which she exhibited in a setting in which the emphasis was placed on the process of designing and production, with all its faults and failures. The visitor, who usually sees only the end product, was thereby given a closer look at the entire production cycle.

Despite (or thanks to) the success of this project, Torres decided to take these ideas even further. So she enrolled at the London College of Fashion where she graduated with the project *An Impossible Wardrobe for the Invisible*. In this project she further developed the theme of 'transience' with 'temporary clothing' with clothing made from fabrics that dissolve in water. In many religions water has a purifying function, in both the literal and the spiritual sense. In her work, water also assumes the function of designer. When the fabrics have dissolved, all that remains are the seams and the memories of the clothing. And the video recording that was made of it.

Lara Torres

Lara Torres (1977, Póvoa de Santa Iria, Portugal) studied to become a worker in precious metals at the Antonio Arroio Art School in Lisbon and then trained as a metalworker with the Austrian jeweller Stephen Maroschek. She became interested in fashion, took a course at the CITEX in Porto, graduated in 2004 and won an internship with Alexander McQueen that same year. In 2005 she began working on projects on the cutting edge of fashion, art, video and performance. Lara Torres teaches Experimental Fashion Design at the Escola Superior de Artes e Design in Caldas da Rainha in Portugal and is a PhD student at the University of the Arts in London.

www.laratorres.com

1977

F

● Portugal

Exhibition

— *An Impossible Wardrobe for the Invisible*
2011
Video installation, inkjet prints
4 photographs: 60 × 40 cm
Video: 28 minutes and
18 seconds
Courtesy of the artist Lara
Torres and the Calouste
Gulbenkian Foundation

A   *An Impossible Wardrobe for the Invisible*, inkjet prints, 2011
B   *An Impossible Wardrobe for the Invisible*, video stills, 2011

Adele Varcoe

1980

F

■ Australia

Adele Varcoe (1980, Melbourne, Australia) is an artist whose main interest is the psychology of fashion. In 2003 she studied for one year at the University of Professional Education in Utrecht, did an internship with Bernhard Willhelm in 2004 and earned her master's degree in fashion design from RIMT University in Melbourne in 2009. From 2006 to 2011 she taught architecture and design at RIMT University, where she is now working on her PhD at that university with research on *The Merging of Clothing and the Body*. She also works as a visiting practitioner at the University of Arts in London.

www.adelevarcoe.com

Exhibition
— *Imagining Chanel*, 2012
— *Participatory Fashion Show*, 2014, performance and video documentations

Fashion, clothing, language, imagination: for Adele Varcoe all these things are related and there's quite a bit of mutual influence as well. When does clothing become fashion? How do we experience clothing and fashion if we don't see the garments but only hear them described in words? Is it the same for everyone? And does fashion really exist, or is it only something that happens in our heads? *The Emperor's New Clothes,* the famous fairy tale by Hans Christiaan Andersen, is an almost inescapable source of inspiration for the conceptual artist Varcoe, but the work of the sociologist Yuniya Kawamura also strikes a chord with her. 'Fashion does provide extra added values to clothing, but the additional elements exist only in people's imaginations and beliefs. Fashion is not visual clothing but is the invisible elements included in clothing.'[1]

Since 2010 Varcoe has been examining the relationships between clothing, language and imagination in a series of marvellous performances. At first glance the performances seem to resemble ordinary fashion shows, but they raise fundamental questions about clothing, both with the public and with those who are showing the clothes.

A

B

A *Catwalk Fash Mob*, Melbourne, 2013. Photography: Peter Burke
B *Imagining Chanel*, Sydney, 2012. Photography: Alex Davies
C *Imagining Chanel*, London, 2012. Photography: Maximiliano Dugnani

The performance *newfangled fashion*, also known as *ifold*, which took place in Melbourne in 2011, had to do with the extent to which the people around us influence the way we experience our own clothing. A narrow catwalk was created in the seclusion of a small tent. 'Models' from the ordinary public walked up and down the catwalk in their everyday clothing, but the public on both sides of the catwalk were naked. Yet as later interviews revealed, it was mainly the models on the catwalk who experienced the situation as exciting, almost as if they had been undressed instead of the spectators.

In *Imagining Chanel*, performed in London and Sydney in 2012, Varcoe played a similar game with the public, who were sitting at tables scattered through the hall. A woman's voice talked about the splendid creations designed by Chanel. Meanwhile, naked models moved elegantly between the tables, stopping every now and then and posing as if they were actually wearing the clothing that the voice was describing. Actors sitting among the spectators entered into conversations about the quality of Chanel's designs and the mannequins. Once again there was that link: what are you seeing and what can you add to it by means of your imagination?

1   See www.adelevarcoe.com/#!imagining-chanel/cl3ea

c

Lilia Yip

1978

F

● Singapore

Lilia Yip (1978, Singapore) began her fashion label in 2010 after having earned her master's degree in Womenswear from the Royal College of Art in London. In her designs Yip combines the wearable with the surreal and the conceptual, taking pleasure in exposing the presuppositions about fashion that are commonly held in our society. Yip uses only sustainable and natural materials, which she obtains from local manufacturers – Lilia Yip lives and works in Brighton, England – in order to support small businesses. Besides the work for her own label Lilia Yip teaches at the University of Brighton and has participated in several exhibitions.

www.liliayip.com

Exhibition
— *Cup of Tea Dress*
  Hand to Heart Dress
  Sing collection
  autumn/winter 2011-2012
  Digital photographic print
  on double Georgette silk,
  bamboo silk
  90 × 60 cm and 85 × 60 cm
— *Facade Dress*
  2012
  Polyester sheen jersey
  110 × 60 cm

'Let your heart speak to other hearts. Embrace the new, remember the old and love all the spaces in between' is the message of the *Sing* collection from autumn/winter 2011-2012 by Lilia Yip. Yip's aim is to draw attention to the worrisome aspects of our society, and she does this in a poetic way. By singing the catwalk music herself – Yip makes her own music for every collection – she creates an intimate world where fashion is not the greatest good, a central theme in her work. For *Sing*, Lilia Yip sought inspiration in Stephen Chow of Hong Kong, who made a few surrealistic comedies back in the 1990s. The collection consists mainly of the colours black, grey and white, and the designs contain trompe-l'oeil photo prints in this colour palette. The design that was selected for the exhibition *The Future of Fashion is Now* is the *Cup of Tea Dress*, a dress made of bamboo silk with a digital photo print of a man's torso with arms and a head, tea in hand.

This humour and agility, often with surrealistic influences, can be found in every Lilia Yip collection, and the same is true of the longing to make more of fashion than just an aesthetic product. This has inspired Lilia Yip to draw up four statements that constitute the guiding principles of her design process: 1. Fashion is a language as well as a form of activism, 2. Collaboration promotes new ways of thinking, making, representing and consuming, 3. Imagination, intelligence and integrity are essential, and beauty and humour are much appreciated, 4. Build up an ethical design practice that respects people, materials and other resources. These principles have led Yip to work exclusively with sustainable and natural materials such as organic cotton, bamboo, silk and wool. All this, combined with an in-depth knowledge of how fabrics should be cut and draped on the body so they move with the body in a flowing line, has made Lilia Yip a highly talented designer with a signature all her own.

A *Cup of Tea Dress* and
   Hand to Heart Dress,
   autumn/winter 2011-2012.
   Exhibition *Lilia Yip* at the
   Night and Day Gallery in
   Singapore.
   Photography: Timothy Lloyd

Fashion Activism: Community and Politics

José Teunissen

The designers in the fourth theme are interested in how far fashion and clothing projects can be enlisted in addressing social themes and how they can contribute to the emancipation of certain target groups or of the consumer. Up until recently it was mainly artists who were involved in this area, people such as Barbara Kruger and Hélio Oiticica. But now more and more fashion designers are also taking an interest in the social and political impact of fashion and clothing because it is a vital way of focusing attention on the fundamental cultural values of fashion and clothing. It is significant that three of the six designers who were commissioned to produce works for *The Future of Fashion is Now* are occupied with this theme.

One of the first fashion designers to demonstrate the persuasiveness of clothing with regard to social issues is the duo Lucy + Jorge Orta (United Kingdom, Argentina). With *Nexus Architecture* (1998-2010) they literally created new social ties within a city by zipping together the clothing of separate individuals. The individuals, taken together, formed a new social network. This is Lucy + Jorge Orta's way of criticising today's anonymous urban culture. Unquestionably, Jorge Orta's South American background influenced the nature of the work. Indeed, South and Central America have a long tradition of political and activist art in which the body and its clothing are used as a medium, with the Brazilian performance artist Hélio Oiticica as the great inspiration. In the youngest generation it was perfectly natural for fashion designer Lucía Cuba (Peru) and artist Tania Candiani (Mexico) to elaborate on this theme as well.

'My work constitutes a critical approach to fashion

design and the construction and exploration of garments as performative and political devices. I am interested in broadening the understanding of the role of fashion design objects, from purely functional or aesthetic considerations, to social, ethical and political perspectives. My work is driven by the desire to harness the agency of clothes and question the established language of fashion, as experienced today, and by the attempt to broaden the potential grammars of critical action through clothes, both as wearable devices and as affective and *embodied cultural media*,' says Lucía Cuba.[1] After having trained to be a social scientist, she then studied fashion at Parsons in New York. With fashion and clothing as *embodied cultural media* she addresses areas of social unrest and abuses in contemporary South American society. With her project *Artículo 6* (2012) Cuba decried the fact that between 1996 and 2000 more than three hundred thousand women and sixteen thousand men were forcibly sterilised in Peru. The project consists of thirty-four articles of clothing on which have been embroidered texts and references to Artículo 6 –

Lucía Cuba, *Artículo 6*, visual essay *La Espera* (*The Waiting*), 2013

the section of the law that justified this action – as well as twelve 'actions' in the form of performances and exhibitions. For *Exercises on Health* (2014), the project that Cuba developed especially for *The Future of Fashion is Now*, she goes even further down this path and examines the theme of 'health'. She thinks too much is being said in terms of 'patient' and 'victim', and that too little attention is paid to the experience of health and illness. 'Because health can sometimes be elusive, hidden behind the mind or a body and silenced by uncertainty, I use garments to explore the felt but unsaid: the affective surplus of a diagnosis that does not withstand the complexity of human emotions and representations.'[2]

With *Exercises on Health* she tries by means of clothing to clarify how human beings relate to health and life. '*Exercises on Health* are garment-based approaches to human encounters with health and life, as seen from the hardships that a place and experience of health can bring forth', says Cuba.[3]

Tania Candiani often chooses a physical site as the point of departure for her work, preferably a specific place, a junction where life takes place, a network in which social ties reveal themselves. For the project *La Constancia Dormida* (2006) Candiani moved her studio to a bankrupt textile factory

Tania Candiani, *La Constancia Dormida*, 2006

for a period of thirty days. She set herself the goal there of making one dress a day. Each dress functioned as a sort of page from a diary in which anecdotes were embroidered from the time that the factory was still active, mixed with stories from visitors who dropped in to see Candiani. Thus by means of the dresses Candiani not only made the history of this factory tangible, with its harsh working conditions, but she also exposed the nostalgia of the former workers and those who lived nearby. 'Textiles have been present in my work as tailoring, as a narrative resource and as labour, socially embedded with meaning. Tailoring as design is a contact point with architecture, where the space distribution of the plans as sewing patterns re-signifying the idea of inhabited space or the utopia of an space that could be inhabited.'[4] In this project, the clothing refers to a social network on the one hand, but it also makes the daily practice of life in this factory more tangible.

In other fashion projects shown in the exhibition that have a political and activist slant, criticism is primarily directed at the rigidity of the fashion system, which constantly stimulates faster production and more consumption and is aimed at turning the passive consumer into an active, independent consumer. Because of the power of the mega-brands there's hardly any room left for small brands and young designers. In addition, cheap chain stores such as H&M and Zara have killed off do-it-yourself fashion, which was still quite common in the 1970s: making one's own clothes has become much more expensive than buying a garment that is produced far away. With that idea in mind, all sorts of citizen initiatives have sprung up since the beginning of the twenty-first century that actively involve the consumer in the process of making clothing. Usually these kinds of projects are initiated by young designers.

D&K – Ricarda Bigolin and Nella Themelios, *#thathautecouture feeling*, 2013

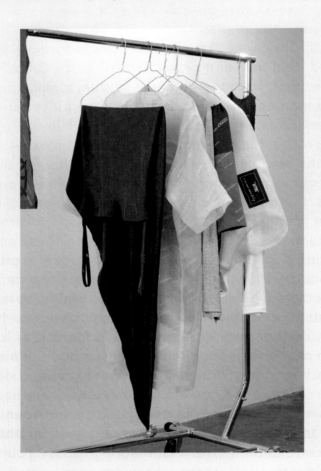

There are initiatives, for example, in which contributed clothing is restyled by young designers into something different (*up-cycling*), and *repair workshops* where designers learn how clothing can be repaired instead of being thrown away.[5] More and more designers are realising that these kinds of fashion projects, in which they serve as director and assume an activist role, can contribute to social cohesion and the capacity of ordinary citizens to participate, while at the same time they break down the power of consumerism and big business –

or at least expose it. With this idea in mind, Ricarda Bigolin and Nella Themelios (Australia) developed *Brand Illusions* (2012) under the name D&K, a fake commercial brand in which a series of activist installations are used to make the viewer aware of all the facets of brand identity. What is the essence of a brand and how does it function typographically in the media? For *The Future of Fashion is Now*, D&K developed *Hardly Brand – Softer Sell* (2014), an installation that examines a brand's limitations. A fashion label creates a gorgeous imaginary world by means of shows and lovely campaigns, but when the consumer has the actual product in hand he or she is often disappointed because the garment isn't well-made and the magical aura of the campaign has completely disappeared. 'The project aims to foreground the awkward "realities" and brutal "truths" of the diffusion process in fashion: from the highly desirable, idealised and constructed moments in catwalk show to their inevitable and disappointing diffusion into saleable products.'[6] In this way the duo hope to reveal the discrepancy between the expectations aroused by the brand and the actual garment, thereby showing that the consumer is longing for new values in the production process. In these values the imagination is inextricably linked to the product, as it is in the *slow fashion* movement.[7]

'The image, the imagined, the imaginary – these are all terms that direct us to something critical and new in global cultural processes: the imagination as a *social practice*,' states the sociologist Arjun Appadurai.[8] According to him, the imagination is no longer being employed in our contemporary globalised culture as a materialised fantasy, as a form of escapism or as a reflection of another world: '… the imagination has become an organized field of social practices, a form of work (in the sense of both labor and culturally organized practice), and a form of negotation between sites of agency (individuals) and globally defined fields of possibility.'[9] He is convinced that the imagination in today's culture must search for new values that are linked with culture and social practice. The project *Pure hearts make truly new and infinite things. Nothing is impossible for a faithful heart, faith moves mountains* (2014) that Dooling Jiang (China) developed for *The Future of Fashion is Now* is a fine example of this. She regards fashion as an 'honest reflection of human longings' and craftsmanship as a crucial link: 'craftmanship perfectly tells the truly "new" of man's authentic objectiveness which could break through the emotionless mechanical production at present. Under this foundation, "new" is infinite.' In the

Chinese tradition, craftsmanship is the perfecting of a product by making it over and over again. Whereas the West tends to focus on the new, the Chinese recognise the power of repetition, because – just as in nature – endless repetition naturally gives rise to the new, 'from aspects of historical stratification and the range of our daily activity. In China both aspects have a rich tradition. The people in the countryside believe very

Digest Design Workshop, *Digest BLUEGround*, ready-to-wear collection, spring/summer 2014. Photography: Qiananrchy

strongly that we "must live in harmony with our native soil" (a central value). Fashion is a combination of human longings; what I want to contribute to the current fashion system is to expose the purest relationship between the human individual and fashion, as well as to examine the universal value of this relationship.'[10] The imagination and new values emanate from the rich history and heritage of Chinese culture and its social connections. But as Nicolas Bourriaud says, they are translated into a universally readable image and fashion language in order to address the public with a number of important questions about the future. How do we want to relate to the things that surround us? What gives value to our lives, and how important is our community and our culture in this regard?[11]

156

The extraordinary thing about our globalised world today is that a wide range of cultures show us the different essences and strengths of something that we wear every day, that we regard as quite ordinary and usually look at through high-fashion commercial glasses.

1 See www.luciacuba.com
2 E-mail correspondence with the artist about the commission.
3 *Ibid.*
4 See www.taniacandiani.com/cvabout.html
5 Otto von Bush, *Fashion-able: Hactivism and engaged fashion design*, dissertation, University of Gothenburg, 2008.
6 E-mail correspondence with the artist about the commission.
7 *Ibid.*
8 Arjun Appadurai, *Modernity at Large*, Minneapolis 1996, p. 31.
9 *Ibid.*
10 E-mail correspondence with the artist about the commission.
11 See pp. 14-15.

Lucy + Jorge Orta

● United Kingdom + Argentina   F + M   1966 + 1953

Lucy Orta (1966, Sutton Coldfield, United Kingdom) graduated cum laude as a fashion designer from Nottingham Trent University in 1989. In 1991 she met Jorge Orta (1953, Rosario, Argentina), who was trained as a visual artist and architect at the Universidad Nacional de Rosario in Argentina. Because of his work as an artist during the dictatorship of the Videla regime, Jorge Orta became very aware of the social role of art. This awareness became the driving force behind their collaboration in Studio Orta. They put together installations, performances and other art projects in which the focus is on social relationships and the way human beings influence nature. The work of Lucy + Jorge Orta is exhibited in galleries and museums all over the world and has been published in a series of monographs.

www.studio-orta.com

Exhibition
— *Nexus Architecture x 25
  – Nexus Type Opera.tion*
  2001
  25 Nexus overalls; microporous polyamide, silkscreen print, zippers, wooden supports
  Max. 600 × 600 × 200 cm
— *Wandering*, 2009
  Video: 16 minutes, 30 seconds

The meeting of Lucy and Jorge Orta in 1991 brought about a great change in both their lives. Lucy was working in Paris as a stylist for trend bureaus and designers at the time, but she became interested in the social and political engagement that she saw in the work of Jorge Orta, an Argentinean exile living in Paris. They decided to work together under the name Studio Orta, where they would address all sorts of social and political questions through the medium of art. Like Joseph Beuys, they believe strongly in the idea of art as a catalyst for social change, and thus a great many large projects have seen the light of day over the past few decades. Even though Lucy Orta was trained as a fashion designer, the collaborative structure of Studio Orta meant that there were no more limits in terms of materials and media, and any amount of experimentation was welcome: with textile, steel, bronze, glass, video, light and much, much more. The focus was always on the relationship between the individual and the surrounding world, with all its social and ecological implications. The *Habitent* (1992) is both a garment and a tent and is intended as a commentary on the dreadful situation in which the Kurdish refugees in Iraq found themselves, with their lack of clothing and shelter. In *OrtaWater*, which was started in 2005, they created a large number of installations having to do with drinking water, one of the major issues we will be facing in the near future. And in *Antarctica* (2007) they built fifty tents on Antarctica, the only continent that has not been claimed by any nation. The tents were made of flags from different countries and thus were symbolic of the world community without borders. The Antarctic village was completed by a flag planted by Lucy and Jorge which is also made up of a large number of different flags.

Closely related to *Antarctica* is the project *EU-Roma*, in which Studio Orta investigates and exposes the lives of the Roma in Europe. Ever since the Roma left India and Egypt about six hundred years ago they have been wandering throughout Europe, at home both everywhere and nowhere, harassed by national borders and nationalistic ideas that dictate their homelessness and invisibility. The video installation *Wandering* (2009) is part of this project and shows the traditional wide flaring skirts of a woman performing traditional Roma dances to the tunes of equally traditional Roma music. The colourful, flowered skirts were made by Lucy in collaboration with the London College of Fashion. Shazam, the smart phone app that can identify music of almost any kind, does not recognise the Roma music. And so it is with the unknown world that is given a voice and a face by Studio Orta.

Nexus Architecture
To what extent are we individuals and to what extent are we part of a whole, of a collective, of a society? Should we conform, and thus enable the whole to continue functioning? Or should we opt for our own individuality and risk the collapse of the whole – of society? These questions were constantly being raised during the years of the project *Nexus Architecture* (1998-2010), which consisted of a large number of performances in galleries, museums and public spaces. Volunteers were dressed in identical, futuristic-looking bodysuits that were then linked together by means of pieces of fabric or zippers, forming a long snake or a grid. The completely identical clothing and the incorporation of the individual into a preconceived form (the group!) was meant to cancel out the feeling of individuality and perhaps even cause a loss of humanity. It probably was no accident that the project was conceived just when the Iraq war was in full swing and the excesses in places such as the Abu Ghraib prison were gaining worldwide attention. The loss of individuality and humanity was further reinforced when Lucy Orta set the entire piece in motion by blowing on a flute or shouting out commands. Now individuals were reduced to components in a geometrically constructed whole that could only move in the desired direction if everyone went along. A number of the volunteers usually experienced the forced collectivity and uniformity as coercive, unnatural and disturbing. Rebellious groups quickly formed who ignored Orta's orders, while others obediently continued to comply with the instructions. The micro-society that this created has a great deal in common with the society of which we all are a part, including the never-ending tension that exists in every society between conformity and individuality.

A

A   *Wandering*, 2009.
    Photography: Lucy + Jorge Orta
B   *Nexus Architecture x 50
    – Nexus Type Opera.tion*, 2001.
    Photography: Peter Guenzel

B

In her work Tania Candiani investigates the emotional consciousness of a social group and the context within which this consciousness exists. Candiani is fascinated by the way in which processes and places connect aspects of life in a network of organic systems, human practices and cultural institutions. Her goal is to create personal experiences and connections in which images, objects and experiences serve as an interface between people and their shared environment. In addition to the role of the environment, the role of the media in our daily lives is also an important theme in the work of Tania Candiani: how the media have formed our culture and how media images have become part of our identity.

La Constancia Dormida (2006) was first exhibited in a former textile factory in Puebla, Mexico. Candiani's hope was that this work would blow new life into the factory. She did this by using the factory as her sewing and embroidery studio for a period of thirty days, creating a new dress every day. Candiani embroidered a total of about 400 metres of fabric. The thirty dresses can be seen as embroidered diaries in which she tells

Tania Candiani

Tania Candiani (1974, Mexico City, Mexico) studied Spanish literature at the Universidad Nacional Autónoma de México (UNAM). Because of a prolonged strike during her years at the university she was never able to graduate. In 1994 she moved to Tijuana, where she wrote an article about the local art scene for a magazine in Mexico. She met many creative spirits there. Mexico, with its eclectic mix of localism, history, drugs, capitalism, violence, music and beaches, inspired Candiani to make art herself. She was asked to participate in a group exhibition with other artists from Tijuana, most of them self-taught because the city has no art academy. Since then her work has been added to the collections of the Museum of Contemporary Art in La Jolla, California, the San Diego Museum of Art and the Mexican Museum in San Francisco.

www.taniacandiani.com

Exhibition
— *La Constancia Dormida*
  Location-specific installation; various fabrics, threads, metal hooks and sound

F   1974

■ Mexico

A

anecdotes about the time when the factory was still in operation as well as stories about people Candiani visited while she was working there. Her unremitting labour – six days a week and eight hours a day – was her way of honouring the factory, the hard work of the factory workers and the value of the materials they produced. In *The Future of Fashion is Now* an abridged version of *La Constancia Dormida* is on display: five outfits with five metres of embroidered text.

A   *La Constancia Dormida*, installation, 2006.
     Photography: Tania Candiani

A

Hassan Hajjaj grew up in Morocco and moved to London when he was thirteen. After completing school he rolled from one job to another. He worked as a DJ, as an organiser of parties and events, as the owner of a clothing shop, as a designer and as a stylist. Finally, after having become a successful artist and the designer of installations and interiors, he went to Morocco to assist in a fashion photo shoot. It irritated him that his homeland was being used as nothing more than a picturesque, Eastern background for Western fashion and models, and he decided to take a radically different approach in his own photography. He started out mainly with photos of friends and acquaintances that he made for himself and did not want to exhibit. It wasn't until he met gallery owner Rose Issa, who urged him to do something serious with his photography, that he found his own style.

That style relies partly on the work of great African photographers such as Seydou Keïta and Malick Sidibé and also contains Andy Warhol-like elements, but its main goal is to undermine prevailing clichés about the Arab world. Hajjaj's work is a reflection of the clash between traditional Moroccan values and Western culture, a culture whose music, films, food and clothing is thoroughly permeated by every other culture, including Moroccan, which it dismisses as tradition as opposed to its own modernity. How can you preserve your own Moroccan culture while living in Morocco and still be modern? That's the question that Hajjaj seems to be addressing anew in every photo he takes.

For the series *Kesh Angels* he portrayed young Moroccan women – sometimes in the studio, sometimes in the street – who navigate the busy traffic of Marrakesh every day on their scooters and motorcycles, travelling to and from work. Each of them, without exception, is veiled, but they always pose in an attitude that is self-confident and sometimes frankly defiant. Every now and then you even see an intentionally exposed leg. Enriching each of the images and providing them with an extra layer of meaning are the frames that surround them: little boxes featuring soup tins, packs of chicken bouillon, Lego blocks, pots of henna powder, etc., all with Arabic inscriptions.

In an earlier series, *Dakka Marrakesh*, Hajjaj seems to have created classical Eastern fantasies with veiled women and men in Arabic caps. When you look carefully, however, you see that the veils, djellabas and caps are covered with the logos of Western brands like Nike, Gucci and Louis Vuitton, or with expressly modern polka dots and leopard prints. East and West, traditional and modern: in Hajjaj's work they don't contradict but go quite naturally together.

Hassan Hajjaj

Hassan Hajjaj (1961, Larache, Morocco) is a self-taught artist whose work includes photos, installations and interiors for places such as the Andy Wahloo bar in Paris. In 2009 he was dominated for the Jameel Prize, awarded by the Victoria and Albert Museum in London, and in 2011 he received the Sovereign African Art Prize from the Sovereign Art Foundation. His work has been shown in museums and galleries all over the world and can be found in countless public and private collections. Hajjaj lives and works in London and Marrakesh. He is represented by the London gallery Rose Issa Projects.

www.roseissa.com

Exhibition
— *Three Women* (ed. 4/7)
 2002
 Digital print (C-type) on Fuji Crystal Archive paper, frame: walnut, handmade; framed: Arabic cans of Sprite
 93.5 × 136 cm
 Courtesy of Matisse Gallery, Marrakech, Morocco
— *Just Do It in Blue* (ed. 4/10)
 2006
 Digital giclee-print (C-type) on paper, handpainted background; frame: wood and rubber tire
 55 × 65 cm
 Courtesy of Rose Issa Projects, London, United Kingdom
— *Puma Blue Veil* (ed. 2/10)
 2006
 Digital inkjetprint (C-type) on paper, acrylic paint; frame: wood and rubber tire
 55 × 65 cm
 Courtesy of Rose Issa Projects, London, United Kingdom

B

A *Three Women*, 2002.
 Photography: with special thanks to Rose Issa Projects
B *Just Do It in Blue*, 2006.
 Photography: with special thanks to Rose Issa Projects

Lucía Cuba

1980

F

Peru

Lucía Cuba (1980, Lima, Peru) earned a master's degree in psychology and a PhD in public health from the Universidad Peruana Cayetano Heredia in Lima. In 2005 she began studying fashion design at the Centro de Altos Studios de la Moda in Lima, and in 2012 she earned her master's degree in Fashion Design and Society from Parsons The New School for Design in New York. Cuba makes collections, performances and exhibitions having to do with sustainability and development. She is the founder of the design label LUCCO and works as a public health consultant. She also teaches psychology and fashion design. Her work has been awarded many prizes and has been exhibited in Peru, Spain and the United States, among other places.

www.luciacuba.com
www.articulo6.pe

Article 6 of the Peruvian Health Act states that every Peruvian citizen has the right to choose the contraceptive method they prefer, and that in the case of unalterable medical procedures written permission from the patient is always required. Yet in Peru between 1996 and 2000, when President Alberto Fujimori was in office, more than three hundred thousand women and sixteen thousand men were sterilised, either forcibly or under false pretences. Almost all of them came from the poorest parts of the country, areas where very little Spanish is spoken and where the birth and mortality rates are high. Not only did the procedures take place under coercion, but they also were often performed under poor hygienic conditions, which regularly led to complications and in some cases even death. Despite repeated efforts on the part of the victims to bring the case to court, the Peruvian government has consistently succeeded in keeping a lid on the affair.

In *Artículo 6* the fashion designer and social scientist Lucía Cuba addresses these crimes. The project consists of thirty-four different articles of clothing and twelve 'actions': installations, performances, exhibitions, a film, a photo shoot, lectures and workshops. The clothing is inspired by the

traditional *polleras* that are worn in the Andes, which are deconstructed and reinterpreted by Cuba. Texts, images and symbols that refer to article 6 and to the crimes committed by the government are printed on sturdy cotton fabrics in twilled ribbon and canvas.

The project was presented as Cuba's graduation project from Parsons The New School for Design in the spring of 2013 during New York Fashion Week. Soon after the presentation Cuba was approached by Lady Gaga, who wanted to use one of the dresses for the presentation of her new perfume, *Fame*. Although the collection is expressly not intended for commercial use, Cuba agreed: 'The fact that Lady Gaga is wearing the dress is going to make it easier to get the notion of "respect" on the agenda. But it's not about attracting attention. After all, the ultimate goal is that the government recognise the victims and give them the attention they rightfully deserve.'

A *Primero*, *Artículo 6* project,
Action #1, 2012.
Art direction: Lucía Cuba
Photography: Erasmo Wong S.
Model: Carla Rincón for Iceberg

B *Cusco*, *Artículo 6* project,
Action #7, 2013.
Photography: Erasmo Wong S.
Performers: Ana Zúñiga and
Andrea Mejía

Exercises on Health, Part 1

A

Perhaps the most important question that fashion faces today is whether it will settle for a future determined by commercial imperatives, oriented towards the production of commodities for sale, or position itself as a critical tool for the interpretation and transformation of social reality. Will the future of fashion design continue to be structured exclusively by industrial capitalism or will we be able to reclaim design as a fundamental human capacity to give shape to specific social experiences?

Exercises on Health (*EOH*) proposes that fashion can serve as an instrument for the interpretation and transformation of social reality. This work construes fashion design as critical methodology, crafting a series of garments as navigational devices that carry forth an epistemology and a politics for social cognition, one that stands at odds with fashion as a cultural manifestation of late capitalism. The work aims to reclaim design as humanistic and emancipatory practice and garments as media for the symbolic dispute of the body and its experience.

In this project garments stand as materialised experiences, giving new yet familiar form to stories of people confronting health. These new 'bodies' are then worn in diverse social settings, re-enacting subjectivities and underlining the importance of their recognition in different contexts, especially in those that lie outside places where health is supposed to exist. In *EOH* the absence of health is addressed as one of the most human of hardships faced by people all over the world today. At the heart of this project is the proposition that the future of fashion depends on our capacity to reconfigure fashion design as a method for the construction of social

B

forms that interpret and transform social reality, including those having to do with improving health outcomes through prevention and policy.

EOH builds a bridge between fashion as interpretative practice and health as a domain of human experience and emotions. Part 1 of *EOH* – the first stage of a larger and ongoing project – is the consequence of a design process involving fieldwork conducted in Peru, interviews, audiovisual documentation, discourse and garment-based analysis. The result is an installation involving four garments: a set of devices interrelated through form, function and experience, shedding light on the complex universe of affections and significations that is revealed by concerns with health and the body.

The project *Exercises on Health* explores the politics of garments as cognitive devices, the possibility of fashion as creative and political endeavour and the significance of proposing new relationships between fashion and health.

Each of the pieces is a vehicle for one of the four narratives that I gathered during fieldwork in April. Each of the garments carries a personal story and is related to the others. The idea is that these 'individuals' share a common space of affection.

The pieces were made entirely out of handwoven and embroidered cotton thread in red, black, white and pink. Each of the colours defines a singular identity, sharing a common

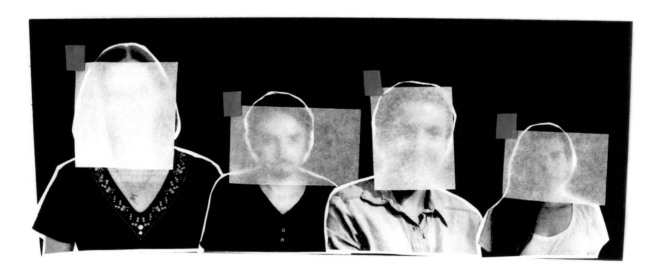

C

A-B-C
Exercises on Health,
Part 1, 2014

D   *Exercises on Health*, Part 1,
    weaving process, 2014

E-F-G-H-I-J-K
    Exercises on Health, Part 1,
    Lima, 2014.
    Photography: Tony Robles
    Art Direction: Lucía Cuba
    Models: Mera De la Rosa,
    Angelique Mumenthaler,
    Paulo Novoa and Estefanía
    Villalobos

D

thread and exploring the location of their health condition through weaving. The selection of the colours is also based on the idea behind colour and identity, and colour and health (for example, in the case of the pink piece there is a specific suggestion of the use of this colour in the fight against a particular type of cancer).

The four pieces show the final stage of the weaving process. They will be completed by placing four small embroidered panels inside each garment as a 'label'.

Lucía Cuba

E

F

G

H

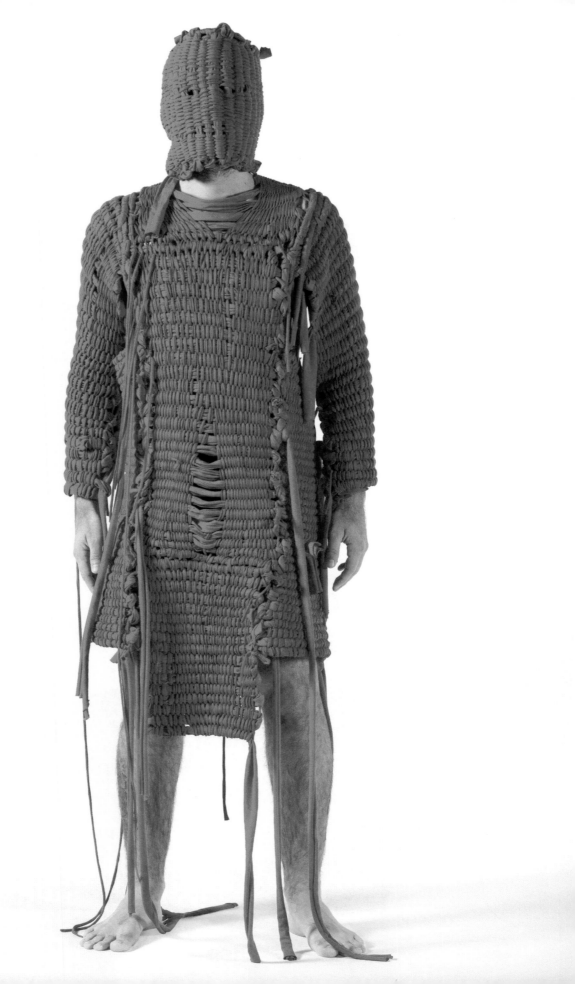

D&K
Ricarda Bigolin and Nella Themelios

1979 + 1977

F + F

■ Australia

Ricarda Bigolin (1979, Melbourne, Australia) earned her bachelor's degree in fashion from RMIT University in Melbourne in 2004. She was a studio assistant at Julie Goodwin Couture, did an internship at BLESS in Paris and worked for two years as a lingerie designer at Simon de Winter in Melbourne. In 2008 she began teaching at RMIT University, where she obtained her PhD in 2012. Since 2013 she has been working with Nella Themelios under the name D&K.

Nella Themelios (1977, Melbourne, Australia) studied art history and exhibition making at the University of Melbourne, where she earned her master's degree in 2013. She worked at Craft Victoria in Melbourne as a coordinating curator and is a member of the management team of the independent art organisation BUS Projects. She is also creative producer at the RMIT Design Hub and is part of the D&K fashion collective.

www.vimeo.com/64474243
www.vimeo.com/64476587

A   B

A   Aftrs/D&K, *effortless beauty takes a lot of effort*, 2013, installation, 2-channel video. Photography: Sampo Pankki

B   Aftrs/D&K, *Aftrs/Dolci & Kabana, from party to bed pulled inky bias satin stuck T-shirt dress*, 2013. Photography: Marc Morel

C   Aftrs/D&K in collaboration with Simon Browne, *Dolci & Kabana Monogram Banner*, 2012

D   Aftrs/D&K in collaboration with Simon Browne, *Dolci & Kabana Monogram Banner*, 2012

No one can fail to notice the irony in the name 'Dolci & Kabana', and even the title of one of their best-known projects, *Brand Delusions*, is hard to misinterpret: don't take fashion brands too seriously, and especially don't let yourself be taken in by the dream world they hold up to you. By doing internships and working for a small, creative fashion label as well as for a number of brands for the general public, Ricarda Bigolin became interested in the world beyond the article of clothing. What is a brand, anyway? How is clothing produced, and how are its artistic values communicated in all the manifestations and products of a particular brand? What is the role of the fashion designer? What is the function of branding and marketing? How do they win you over and give you the illusion that you're part of the world of a certain brand? Under the name D&K, Bigolin and Nella Themelios study the commercial mechanisms that guide daily practice at the big fashion brands. To do this they use performances, installations, films and exhibitions. They call themselves a brand in search of an identity, and in one of their manifestations, the film *Faces* from 2012, that's exactly what happens. Many big fashion brands are represented at some point by a famous face (think of Superman actor Tobey Maguire for Prada, for example, of Kate Moss for Calvin Klein and Oscar-winner Jennifer Lawrence for Dior), so D&K began looking for a face of their own. In a gallery constructed like a temporary film set, the public is invited to take part in a screen test. At the autocue, various sentences appear that literally call up the dream world that fashion brands are often trying to evoke;

the aspirant models are asked to read these sentences aloud. These include statements like 'You look like heaven tonight' or 'Why settle for second best?' At the same time, the models are given instructions on the facial expression and pose they are to assume and how they are to move. All the clichés that are used in fashion photography and brand representation are hauled out, providing insight into how the language of love and longing is exploited by fashion brands. In a work made especially for the exhibition *The Future of Fashion is Now*, D&K goes even further in its investigation of the strategies that fashion brands use to sell their products.

C

D

D&K Hardly Brand –
Softer Sell

1.

Void foam cladding that object of desire
Installing monumental dreams,
cartoon eyes,
Violet crumble crumble,
haute cuisine myths
Honeycomb snowing plate,
foam of honeycomb,
Folds into chocolate in contact with mouth
close your eyes

This transposed texture
transgresses your mind,
Challenge the surface and shape

I always desire a star over a chef's hat
any day,
anyway,

Make a rupture look better.
Blue screen green screen sadness,
Look over your right shoulder
there's a plume of history exhaling
Lined stained plumped coated red lips,
(too many products #stronglook)
Blooming rose gif. Lips,
quiver in monolith salt mine,
Glaze of love glance grazes the dreamy,
not 'broken',
instead shaped ice heart fading in the
'not so strong sun hides in overcast days'
long fall out / drowns out

/smiles
reps./

pause

seconds past
- child's pose

2.

This body of work explores the processes, limitations and invariable disappointments associated with constructing and communicating a convincing 'brand story' in fashion. Branding and marketing statements in this context often circulate as both 'hard' and 'soft' messages, hard and soft 'sells'; clear and strong brand stories as well as customised and subliminal life-style suggestions that subtly depict the experience of being part of and/or with the brand.

D&K Hardly Brand – Softer Sell foregrounds the awkward realities and brutal truths of the diffusion process in fashion: from the highly desirable, idealised and constructed moments in a catwalk show to their inevitable and disappointing diffusion into saleable products.

3.

D&K is a brand in search of an identity – not really a brand or hardly a brand. D&K is in a constant state of 'rebranding', employing strategies of consistently inconsistent messaging. The constituent parts of the 'brand' – name, visual identity, value proposition, target audience – are reconfigured with each project. D&K is characterised by an ongoing investigation into what it means to be 'them' – as a fashion brand and as the persona encoded in such a brand. How does one sustain a brand identity in the tumultuous seas of desire that fuel the conditions of fashion?

In this project, D&K's already contradictory visual identity is further dissolved and distorted. This is a study in obscuring the visual identifiers of a brand. The process mimics a suicide label in music – the typographic iterations begin at the end and regress to zero.

These ideas are explored through the design process, considering different methods to obscure and dissolve branding signatures: cladding, disfiguring, concealing and covering typefaces to distort the integrity, readability and clarity of a logo or 'statement' prints. This process is also

carried through to digital and screen-
printed images and decorative techniques.

4.

Unclear on the stats
Unclear on our identity,
A svelte silhouette glaring glitches in the night,
caressing the neck of another,

A slightly provocative yoga pose
oops,
G-string on the floor coils
sequins,

Small talk
Soft sell
Hard brand
softer sell, from the hardly brand,
The real D&K.
Who are you?
Should we care?

Take this middle finger
I'm waving it to you through the ether,
behind amethyst sequins,
jade jets are nimble at your skin.
Disappointment lingers,
the residue,
that axis subtle around
your hidden days.

Hidden promises,
too subtle to say directly,
too subtle makes ambiguous,
Too directly take risks,
identities glittering in typographic success,
incandescent sculptures.
Kerning that kerns your two souls,
insert placeholder text,

Profits sour,
Celebrity team ups,
People die,
people die metaphorically.
The new coveted one.
2 months of good treatment,
glance over at it,
admire your selection,
keep looking at it,
doubtful about forever.
Not looking for symmetry,
But
I want to get into your hard drive.

misplaced mysticism

Of Ideals to be a great designer,
Minus the vision or follow through,
But 'really good at finding and buying clothes online'.
It's in the post now,
somewhere over the ocean right now.
Plastic smell
Self-sealing parcel,

pro-packed tightly,
synthetic hydrangea,
Or other flowers,
that desire that stays.

You know,
you could take the risk?
With 5-star hotel stays,
Expectation 'love-ins' 'lock-downs'
Keep looking out that window,
Leftover evaporated words,
dinner sessions of re-reading

18 rouge noir
so much black in that red,
Person Chimera,
all the pent up
could be
poetry,
Want this poetry?
a 101 guide
please

5.

D&K 101 T-shirts
A series revealing the multiplicity of the fashion product and the rituals of buying and selling. Featuring Sanja Pahoki's *View from Suomenlinna of the Baltic Sea (Blue)*, 2011.

The ubiquitous printed 'T-shirt' is an iconic form of diffusion in high fashion collections. The T-shirt is often both an entry-level designer garment as well as an overly priced signature style or symbol of a high fashion collection – a seasonal 'must-have'. From bold typographic screen prints to highly embellished seasonal gestures and printed surfaces, the T-shirt varies wildly in both material composition and price.

D&K 101 T-shirts is a study in the trajectory between 'basic' and 'highlight'/ 'directional' and between the integrity of design detail and simplified, printed flat graphics.

Produced in an edition of 101, the series inverts the usual process of production by presenting many slight variations of the one form. In this series, all embellishments, including branding signatures, are removed from the structure of the garment and restored as external additions. The absent branding signatures return as non-integrated accoutrements floating apart from the structural integrity of the garment. The D&K moniker is crossed out, layered, printed over, obscenely modified and transformed. The result is a system of peripheral components/accessories/appendages applied in random sequences to the basic T-shirt form.

The 101 series also reveals a selling process. In this case the 101 T-shirts are all numbered as individual iterations and can be purchased. The act of buying alters the hierarchies of display. The act of buying raises the question: how much would you pay? Does the context, brand signature, trump the material value of such items?

6.

DCK Disappointing Couture
(D&K in collaboration with Chantal Kirby)
A more 'exclusive', high-end subset of
D&K 101 T-shirts.

DCK Disappointing Couture extends the *D&K 101 T-shirts* series, reworking particular edition numbers by adding further garment components. The DCK series uses all of the same componentry as the 101 T-shirts but is highly worked, labour-intensive and luxurious.

DCK Disappointing Couture explores disappointment in fashion – from the failed expectations of buying a garment online to experiencing a garment in reality and being disappointed with its quality. Disappointment is a consequence of desire, or desiring something too much. This idea

is translated into a productive design proposition: masking meaning and falsifying construction by using supplementary and inferior materials and construction techniques that pose as something more delicate and refined.

7.

My shit T-shirt
artful compositions
Everything's fine
Who knows?
Blow out snuff out
nothing

Champagne sparkles eyes
Accidental lies,
tender cheeks
However hopeful
you glance for notifications

Endless image streams
anxious for that turbulent mind
fickle trails of impermanent taste
Tap /
a heart skips red /
my heart floats up red/
Virtual autograph book
on lock screen
One name in all highlight type options
nonchalant heart hides a skipped beat
On the dlo to care IRL
for a split second
the fraction to swipe
for that impulse/
instance
Your image is you
An aptitude for millisecond liking
That always promising after-screen screenglow
Yeah she had that beyond fashion glow

8.

Desire 101
A spoken word audio recording to accompany *D&K 101 T-shirts.*

A text and audio collage that considers the commercialisation of the kind of language that attributes greater sentiment, allure and meaning to a fashion practice. The simplest utterance can add a touch of the 'poetic' – from a verse to a hashtag – and has become prolific in our culture. The work collates quotations, technical language and definitions and fuses this with poetry, questioning the differences between language tropes and gestures of expression when positioned as branding strategies.

D&K – Ricarda Bigolin and
Nella Themelios

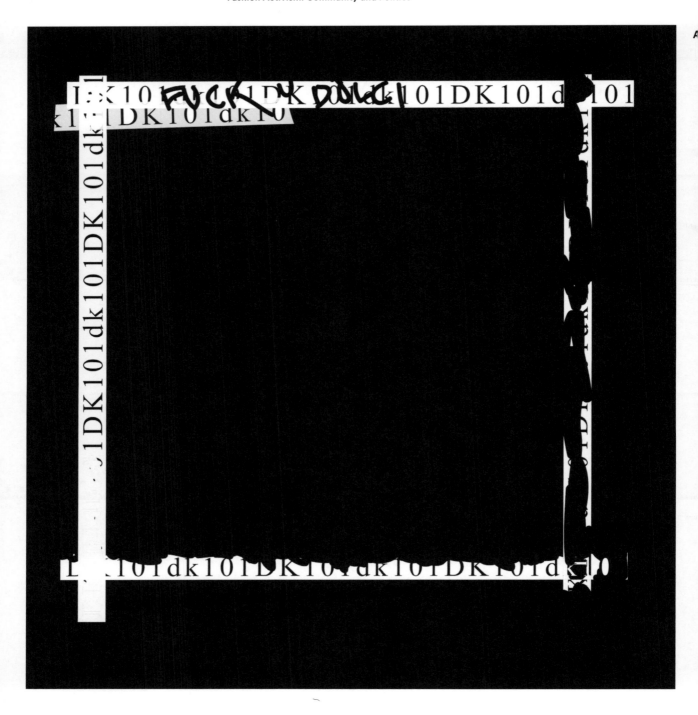

A *D&K 101 T-shirts, Last season's statement frame print*, 2014

B Aftrs/D&K, *DK101 sky camo branding*, 2014 featuring Sanja Pahoki's *View from Suomenlinna of the Baltic Sea (Blue)*, 2011, rotated 90 degrees, medium resolution, with 'D' and 'K' in Bodoni Roman 700 pt camouflaged in the sky

C Aftrs/D&K, *DK101 edition numbers*, 2014 featuring Sanja Pahoki's *View from Suomenlinna of the Baltic Sea (Blue)*, 2011, rotated 45 degrees, low resolution

D *Your Horizon*, 2014

E *Your Horizon*, 2014

D

E

your horizon

Digest Design Workshop
Dooling Jiang

1984

F

● China

Dooling Jiang (1984, Fuzhou (Fujian), China) studied fashion at the Raffles Design Institute in Beijing and continued her education at Central Saint Martins in London in 2008. After returning to China in 2010 she launched her conceptual fashion label Digest Design Workshop, with a ready-to-wear line (Xiao) and a more artistic line (Hua). In 2011 she and Zhang Da took part in the Chengdu Biennale. Jiang and the graphic designer Hou Ying together publish the magazine *Radical Sign*.

www.digest-design.com

The Chinese fashion industry finds itself in a very turbulent phase, caught up in a tangle of past developments. First there's the centuries-old tradition of very wide, loose-fitting clothing, mainly intended to conceal the body. Then there's the legacy of the communist past, when clothing was meant to eliminate any trace of individuality. And now, for the last few decades, there's been a tidal wave of Western values and trends. On the one hand, China is the land where Western companies can go to have their clothing produced at rock-bottom prices. But it's also the land whose nouveau riche have an insatiable appetite for prestigious Western brands like Prada, Louis Vuitton and Gucci. Many Chinese designers, in search of commercial success, have been looking just as longingly to the West and are mainly preoccupied with copying and imitating.[1] The Chinese designer Dooling Jiang, however, is absolutely not interested in commercial success. With her conceptual brand Digest Design Workshop, she wants to make clothing that says something about the world she inhabits: present-day China. 'I feel that, like architects, designers have a responsibility to use their work to comment and reflect on the world around them – they need to project their own point of view. As a result, I decided to develop a collection to illustrate contemporary China.' One of the big

A

B   C

issues dominating Chinese life is the distinction between the city and the countryside. Industrialisation has led many country people to move to the city, and the cities are expanding further and further. Jiang symbolises the cultural invasion in her collection *The Passage* by dipping a series of white garments into blue ink, so that the blue ink increasingly penetrates the white. The use of polycotton, a cotton-polyester blend, also refers to the mixing of rural and urban, of traditional and modern. In other collections she begins with geometric shapes such as circles and squares, on which she bases loose garments with a boxy fit and an androgynous look, garments that are emphatically modern in terms of cut and material but are also deeply rooted in Chinese traditions. Jiang is convinced that even the Chinese people who are now opting for luxurious Western brands will eventually develop a style more in keeping with Chinese traditions: 'The people who buy my clothes have a lot of experience with these kinds of [Western, ed.] brands. Now, they prefer independent brands such as Digest. They find it more real, and the style might fit them better.'[2]

1   See the digital publication: Erik Bernhardsson, 'Modes China', *De Rigueur*, 2, no. 5, spring 2013, Kindle edition.
2   *Ibid.*

A-B-C
The Passage, collection
for the artistic line (*Hua*),
autumn/winter 2011-2012

Pure Hearts Make Truly New And Infinite Things
Nothing is impossible for a faithful heart,
faith moves mountains

'*He who attends daily to learning increases in learning.
He who practices Tao daily diminishes himself. Thus he attains to non-doing. He practices non-doing and yet there is nothing left undone.*'[1]

Being a young Chinese designer, my statement may represent the attitude of the young generation towards fashion, and I hope that what I am trying to show here will be effective. China has a rich heritage that is reflected in both its long history and its broad engagement in everyday life. The people living in China are strongly tied to a faith in 'living together with our native land' (a core spirit). Thousands of years have gone by and the faith never dies, though the tide of modernisation has pushed this nation to broad diversification over the past hundred years. The remaining social system is unique, and it poses a real dilemma: in China, fashion as a concept cannot be understood in typical Western terms. However, fashion as a phenomenon does exist, no matter what backgrounds we explore. What makes fashion possible is desire. Fashion is an aggregation of man's desire. Therefore, what I hope to contribute to the current fashion system is to uncover the purest relationship between men and fashion and to discuss the universal value of this relationship.

Fashion is always an honest reflection of human desire. Human desire can be boundless, but the world need not comply with it. The world is actually built by means of real manual labour, thus the value of the craftsmanship imparted by craftsmen and literati is precious by any standard. Craftsmanship perfectly conveys what is truly 'new' about man's authentic objectivity, which could break through today's emotionless mechanical systems of production. With this foundation, 'new' is infinite. In this project, I will continue working along this path to express that 'new'.

1   Laozi, *Tao Te Ching*, chapter 48

Repetition brings energy

As a designer, especially at a time like the present – 150 years since the arrival of industrialisation and modernisation – aren't there more critical tasks to undertake than the constant 'designing' of new products? Reflecting on our actions, for instance. Reflecting on development, innovation and the speed of construction; reflecting on integrity, mentality and the stability of our constructions. Within the context of the contemporary industry, the designing of garments, we question whether the fashion industry is the only road to travel. Are designs based on the four seasons of nature inferior to six-month fashion trends? The four seasons are cyclical, like wheels moving forward, like tree rings,, and even the planet cannot stop spinning on its own axis and moving forward. The cycle that comes full circle provides space for development in human survival.

China has had more dynasties than almost any other culture, and the thread of its civilisation has never ceased. Its ancient hieroglyphs have been developing for 5000 years, and still live on in the 21st century. Moreover, we still understand the ancients' record of history and culture. The history of Chinese development has been advancing in cycles through the rise and fall of the dynasties, in the spring and autumn, with the warring states, the separations and wars during The Five Dynasties and Ten States, thus the Qin and Han Dynasties, and then to the height of the Tang and Song Dynasties. Even though the emergence of modern science has brought tremendous convenience to people's lives, and the differences between various cultures and nations have narrowed, the individual – the most important component of our world – has not undergone any essential changes in thousands of years.

People still work in the daytime and rest after sunset, consuming three meals daily. Nor have we stopped sleeping regularly, enabling us to maintain our various basic bodily functions. All of these are 'repetitive', and such repetition brings energy, which can also be converted into energy.

Seeking pure hearts
A conceivable and sustainable solution to converting livelihood and environmental issues into fashion design

In my commissioned work I focus on presenting the craftsman's excellent carving skill to support my design concept. It is a simple but very strong beginning to practising the various forms of art. In my opinion, this kind of hand carving should be defined as a 'new' technology since it has the ability to change itself over time. For us, this technology is not difficult to learn or to use. The only requirements are patience and a peaceful heart. Impatience is a disease of modern society, especially in cities. Is it better to gain a traditional skill than to be educated or trained at a school or factory?

The pattern is not only a simple story that describes an annual event of the birds coming to feast when the plum tree blossoms, but it also has a symbolic meaning. A play on the phrase 'xi shang mei shao' means happiness appears on the eyebrows. You might wonder what a facial expression has to do with plum blossoms and birds. The bird is a *pica pica* (magpie). Climbing the plum tree ('xi shang mei que') has the same pronunciation as this uncontrollable joy.

The design process starts with traditional elements. The first step is to recompose the pattern panel, transforming the white background with blue flowers to a blue background with white flowers. Then you start carving on oil paper.

I thought I would make the figure and ground in opposing colours. It's quite simple and takes just one second on the computer. I collaborate with craftsmen in the design of these blue-dyed garments. When the craftsman Mr Wang told me doing this by hand carving would be complicated, I was awakened from such naivety. Mr Wang also told me that no one has ever tried to invert the traditional form from white background to blue background in the history of blue cloth manufacturing, so he too is looking forward to seeing the results.

At the moment, the summer of 2014, this research work has resulted in the ready-to-wear collection *Digest BLUEGround*. I hope the wearer will regain his/her ability to communicate with nature through the frugality and humility of the fabric, and will enjoy the experience of the cotton garments.

A-B-C-D
Digest BLUEGround, material and design process, ready-to-wear (*Xiao*) collection, spring/summer 2014. Photography: Qiananrchy

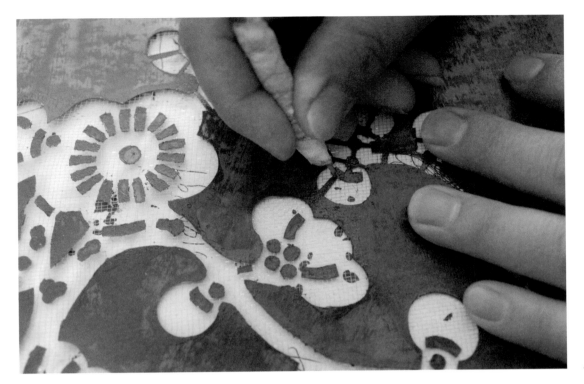

A

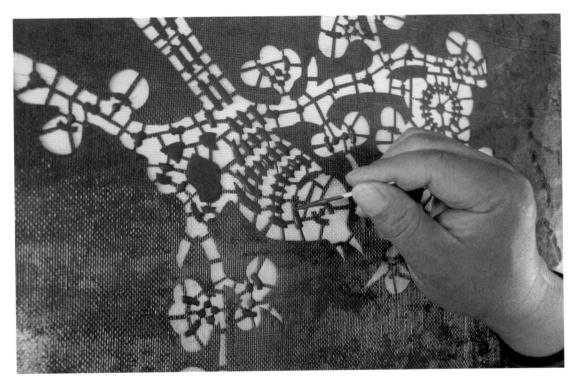

B

布幅60cm

此处图样需补全

图样高度60cm

做成蓝地白花

C

E

F

G

E-F *Digest BLUEGround*,
ready-to-wear
(*Xiao*) collection,
spring/summer 2014.
Photography: Qiananrchy
G Brand Tag *Digest
BLUEGround*, 2014

Our Home
Pure things are vanishing every day; still I am paying my regards to them

This exhibition concept stems from the doubts that arise from the narrative 'Modern technology is the power to speed the progress of civilisation.' I am asking if there is another direction for evolution or a more sustainable path to follow.

The leading direction of the revolution of modern society relies on industrial economic principles, so that many traditional customs that do not benefit the economy have faded in recent years. Referring to Zygmunt Bauman's book *Modernity and the Holocaust*, in order to picture the progress of this century's evolution it might be appropriate to examine the concept of modernity.

I decided on several fabrics that are present only in certain areas of China in order to demonstrate the traditional production techniques in the exhibition after I finished my research. According to archaeological study, these fabrics have a long history running from 1000 to 3000 years and are believed to have served as important identity symbols and household goods in the lives of local people.

Li brocade from Hainan Island; Miao shiny indigo-dyed cloth from Guizhou; grass linen from Rongchang, Sichuan; Pulu wool from South Tibet; Atlas silk from Hotan, Xinjiang; gambiered Canton gauze from Shunde, Guangdong; blue cloth from Nantong, Jiangsu and Tussah silk from Nanyang, Henan. Some of these come from mainland China, like silk and ramie, while some combine Chinese textile culture with ethnic minority people, like Tibet wool and Li cotton. The tent is the oldest way of building a shelter. The idea of 'Our Home' is to awaken the life experience in our deep memory and to build a bridge between the past and the future. I believe that our life experience is the best inspiration for fashion.

The range of fabrics I have chosen contains mostly natural fibres, dyeing technology and weaving technology that I've known about from tradition. Textile development is an excellent reflection of human society's evolution through ancient times. Studying traditional fabric-making shows us the old spirit we have lost in modern industrial society.

Fashion always presents the everyday life of our times. To the question of whether there is another direction for evolution or a more sustainable way to go, my answer is: to guard our home.

Limited cutting means freedom

Eastern people are good at cutting clothes along straight lines. There are no darts in the clothes, not even any curves. They prefer to follow the scales and proportions that were set by their ancestors. I did a study of minority costumes and fabrics, and then retraced the patterns of the clothing. When I finished the toiles that were derived from these flat clothes, I found that aspects like 'age', 'sex' and 'styles' had simply vanished. The clothes are totally free.

The Netherlands' embankment
Nothing is impossible for a faithful heart, faith moves mountains

The Netherlands is a nation famous for reclaiming the land from the sea. I've heard a story that the amount of stones used by the Dutch people to fill the sea is as many as those used to construct the Great Wall. In the 13th century the seawater began eroding the national territory of the Netherlands, so the Dutch people declared a war on the sea that lasted for several centuries. Now the nation has an 1800-km embankment, having reclaimed 560,0000 ha from the sea. It is a great achievement in the history of the world. The Chinese people even praise it. It is like Jingwei's Filling the Sea, which is a symbol of dogged determination in China.

The theme of this commission is a tent that needs to be fixed on two sides by weights. Thinking of the Dutch people's great achievement, I can imagine what 'home' means to you. For 700 years, you constantly filled the sea with stones. It is the same for the Chinese people. We never stop fighting floods. From King Yu's flood control to Li Bing's Dujiang Dam, we have used our intelligence to fight for a better life. So I think it is important to get the Dutch people involved in this project. The stones from the Netherlands and the tent from the remote eastern nation of China will work together to reflect the same spirit of protecting our home. As a Chinese saying goes: when water flows, a channel is formed.'

Digest Design Workshop – Dooling Jiang

Postscript: Due to the limited time frame my study for this exhibition only covers certain areas in mainland China. In the future, I plan to study how the traditional dress culture could be revived in the modern context, not only in China but throughout the world.

H   Sketch for the *Our Home*
     installation, 2014
I   *Our Home* prototypes, 2014.
     Photography: Qiananrchy

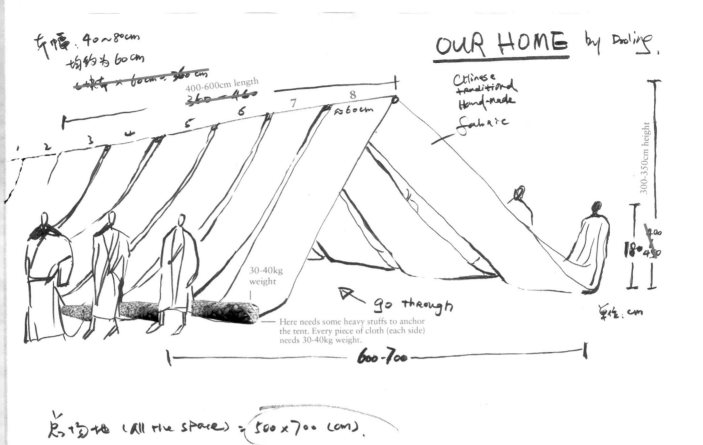

OUR HOME by Dooling.

Chinese traditional Hand-made fabric

400-600cm length

300-350cm height

30-40kg weight

Here needs some heavy stuffs to anchor the tent. Every piece of cloth (each side) needs 30-40kg weight.

go through

600-700

(All the space) = 500 × 700 (cm).

Catalogue published to coincide with the exhibition of the same name in Museum Boijmans Van Beuningen, 11 October 2014 – 18 January 2015.

Concept and editorial supervision
José Teunissen
Jan Brand

Authors
José Teunissen
Han Nefkens
Jos Arts
Hanka van der Voet

Editing
Lucy Klaassen
Esmee Postma

Editorial coordination
Annelies ter Brugge

Images
Andrea Kristić

Translation Dutch – English
Nancy Forest-Flier

Production
Sabine Terra

Design and layout
Glamcult Studio

Printing and lithography
Drukkerij Die Keure, Brugge

Special thanks
Henk Christophersen
Anna E. Kruyswijk

Scouts
H.C. Ali Ansari
Vandana Bhandari
Patricia Brien
Otto von Busch
Síle de Cléir
Paula da Costa Soares
Lucía Cuba
Robyn Healy
Valérie Lamontagne
Ezra Mabengeza
Thando and Vanya Magaliso
Sayoko Nakahara
Nien Siao
Vassilis Zidianakis

Jury
Viktor Horsting
Han Nefkens
Rolf Snoeren
Karin Swerink
José Teunissen
Vassilis Zidianakis

Cover
Concept and art direction:
Glamcult Studio
Photography: Jouke Bos
Styling: Maaike Staal
Hair and make-up: Liselotte van Saarloos
Model: Sophie Vlaming

© 2014 Museum Boijmans Van Beuningen, Rotterdam / the designers, authors and photographers

ISBN 978-90-6918-281-0

This publication is also available in Dutch: ISBN 978-90-6918-280-3

Publisher
Museum Boijmans Van Beuningen
Museumpark 18-20
3015 CX Rotterdam
T +31 (0)10 4419400
F +31 (0)10 4360500
The Netherlands
info@boijmans.nl
www.boijmans.nl

The publication and the exhibition were made possible in part by:

Han Nefkens
Fashion on the Edge

Boijmans Business Club

stimuleringsfonds creatieve industrie

PRINS BERNHARD
CULTUURFONDS

BankGiroLoterij

kfHein,fonds

Stichting Bevordering van Volkskracht